A Humanist Vision

A Humanist Vision

The Adolph Weil, Jr. Collection of Rembrandt Prints

Hilliard T. Goldfarb

Hood Museum of Art, Dartmouth College
1988

© 1988 by the Trustees of Dartmouth College
All rights reserved

Hood Museum of Art
Dartmouth College, Hanover, NH 03755

Library of Congress Cataloguing in Publication Data

Goldfarb, Hilliard T.
   A humanist vision.

   Bibliography: p.
   1. Rembrandt Harmenszoon van Rijn, 1606–1669—
Exhibitions. 2. Etching, Dutch—Exhibitions. 3. Etching
—17th century—Netherlands—Exhibitions. 4. Weil,
Adolph—Art collections—Exhibitions. 5. Etching—
Private collections—Alabama—Montgomery—Exhibitions.
I. Hood Museum of Art. II. Title.
NE2054.5.R4A4   1987   769.92′4   87–26267

DESIGN: *Joyce Kachergis*

TYPESETTING: *Heritage Printers, Inc.*

Cover/jacket illustrations:
FRONT: Rembrandt van Rijn, *Christ Preaching ('La Petite Tombe')*, c. 1652 (cat. no. 58)

BACK: Rembrandt van Rijn, *The Windmill*, 1641 (cat. no. 66)

Photo credits: All photographs of the Weil collection: Scott Photographic Services. Other figure illustrations in this catalogue were reproduced with the permission of the following institutions, cited in the text: Bibliothèque Nationale, Paris; The British Museum, London; Fogg Art Museum, Harvard University, Cambridge, Massachusetts; Réunion des Musées Nationaux (Louvre), Paris; Rijksmuseum, Amsterdam; Staatliche Kunstsammlungen, Dresden.

Printed and bound in Japan

Contents

Preface

When the new Hood Museum of Art opened at Dartmouth College in the fall of 1985, the curators and director of the museum were delighted to learn the extent of interest in collecting art on the part of Dartmouth alumni. One after another, Dartmouth collectors contacted us or were brought to our attention by those who share our belief in the power of art to convey truth and to give pleasure. Our first formal acknowledgment of this interest was the fall 1987 exhibition *From Titian to Sargent: Dartmouth Alumni and Friends Collect*. Others will follow.

One of our alumni has developed a collection so notable in its scope and importance that we felt it warranted a special exhibition of its own. Moreover, the focus of his collection—old master prints—complements an emphasis of Dartmouth's own collecting history. From the 1930s through the 1950s the director of the Dartmouth Art Galleries, Churchill P. Lathrop, stretched his modest acquisition budget by purchasing prints of high quality and interest for teaching purposes. Through his energy and influence, as well as that of the late Ray Nash, Dartmouth has acquired a considerable reputation as a place where the graphic arts are valued.

In addition, gifts of important print collections from Dartmouth alumni and friends such as Frederick Hirschland, Helena M. Wade, and Mrs. Hersey Egginton furthered the growth of the collection in areas important to teaching the history of European art. And in honor of the dedication of the new museum in 1985, the Dartmouth class of 1935 established a Class of 1935 Memorial Fund for the further development of the College's print collection.

It gives us great pleasure, therefore, to share with the Dartmouth community the remarkable collection of Rembrandt prints developed over the past twenty years by Adolph Weil, Jr., a member of the class of 1935. Prints by Rembrandt van Rijn form only a part of Mr. Weil's collecting interests, which he discusses with the museum's curator for European art, Hilliard T. Goldfarb, in an interview published in this catalogue. Dr. Goldfarb, who organized the exhibition and wrote this catalogue, was assisted in the preliminary cataloguing of the prints by one of our museum interns, Andrew Schulz of the class of 1986. The result of their work is now available to all in the form of this fine exhibition and catalogue.

Hilliard Goldfarb joins me in thanking Andrew Schulz and others without whom this project could not have been accomplished: Young Dawkins, class of 1972, who first introduced us to the Weil family; Michael Merrow, class of 1985, who helped in so many ways with the manuscript; Rebecca Buck, museum registrar; Evelyn Marcus and Robert Raiselis, who matted and framed the prints and oversaw the installation of the exhibition; our catalogue designer, Joyce Kachergis, and editor, Jess Bell; along with others who helped in ways too numerous to mention here.

Finally, we extend our deep gratitude to the Weil family of Montgomery, Alabama. In particular, we thank Adolph Weil; his wife, Jean; his brother and fellow collector, Robert, class of 1940; Robert's wife, Virginia; sons Adolph I. Weil III and Robert S. Weil II, class of 1973; Wallace Darneille, class of 1973; and the entire extended family at Weil Brothers Cotton. All of them made our visits to Montgomery a source of fond memories of kindness and warm hospitality. Such kindness, I have found, is very much a part of the Dartmouth tradition. It is our privilege to return it in some measure on the occasion of the present exhibition.

JACQUELYNN BAAS
Director

Introduction

Among the responsibilities of the curator for European art at the Hood Museum of Art at Dartmouth College, that of visiting collectors who have an association with Dartmouth is among the most enjoyable and stimulating. Rarely, however, has this experience been as satisfying as in my acquaintance with Adolph Weil, Jr., of the Dartmouth class of 1935. The sensitivity, care, and devotion that Mr. Weil brings to the collecting of old master prints is hardly limited to the genius of Rembrandt. His extensive collection includes marvelous examples, in many cases quite comprehensive, of the graphic work of Mantegna, Dürer, Altdorfer, Lucas van Leyden, Callot, Piranesi, Canaletto, Tiepolo, Goya, David Lucas, Pissarro, Whistler, and Kerr Eby. Over the years he has done far more than acquire the familiarity with print states and impressions that one expects of the serious collector; in his distinctive, understated way, he has become a scholar in the field of old master prints.

In addition to Mr. Weil's private art collection, he and his brother, Robert Weil, class of 1940, have together built a corporate collection of distinction, including fine paintings, sculptures, and works on paper by such outstanding artists as Pissarro, Degas, Monet, Renoir, Cassatt, Rodin, Maillol, Homer, Benton, and Wyeth. The corporation is the family partnership of Weil Brothers Cotton, Inc. of Montgomery, Alabama, to which the brothers returned after service in World War II and graduate degrees at Harvard University, and where they and their sons continue to manage an enterprise begun by their forebears over a century ago.

In the recent exhibition *From Titian to Sargent: Dartmouth Alumni and Friends Collect*, we had the opportunity to exhibit several masterpieces both from Mr. Weil's personal collection and from the corporate collection. It was decided to exclude the Weil Rembrandts from that show and instead to mount a comprehensive exhibition of these prints in conjunction with a catalogue raisonné. Individual impressions from the Adolph Weil print collection had been exhibited at several institutions; however, the quality and breadth of the Rembrandts—some 81 prints, nearly a third of the artist's corpus and representing in depth all the genres of his production—seemed to deserve more. It has been our great pleasure to catalogue, research, exhibit, and publish this important private collection.

The timing of this exhibition was planned to coincide with two courses being taught at the College, an art history survey and a seminar on Rembrandt, thus providing students with an extraordinary opportunity to study original works of the highest quality in connection with their class assignments. The museum also provides professional experience and training for individual students through museum internships. During the 1985–86 academic year, Andrew Schulz, a member of the class of 1986, worked with me on this project. Andrew's exemplary work in conducting a preliminary cataloguing of the collection was of a standard one would expect of a serious graduate student—a testimony both to him and to the opportunities afforded by Dartmouth and the Hood Museum.

In her preface, Jacquelynn Baas expresses her gratitude and mine to the many individuals without whom this exhibition and catalogue could not have been realized. I would also like to add to her list Barbara Reed, Art Librarian at Dartmouth College, and the staff of the Sherman Art Library, especially Marilyn Gasser, Jean Hill, and Claudia Yatsevitch, for their smiling and unfailing assistance.

The title of this catalogue originated with a statement of Mr. Weil, recorded in our interview, concerning his mother's admiration of Rembrandt and his own early attraction to the artist's work. The humanism that underlies Rembrandt's art is a profound truth of which one becomes repeatedly aware in considering the organization of his compositions, his choice of narratives, his selection and adaptation of visual sources, his stylistic development, and the effects he sought in the technical manipulation of the etching plate. This humanism was nurtured by his Calvinist and Mennonite religious ambience, the cosmopolitan culture of Amsterdam, the development of empiricism and scientific method in the seventeenth century, and the personal dimensions of his life. It is a characteristic that extends even to Rembrandt's landscapes, tied as they are to actual observations of the Dutch countryside, including people and their dwellings, labors, and activities. It has ensured the artist's unabated appreciation to the present day.

Printmaking was clearly a primary means of artistic expression for Rembrandt. He was not only the greatest etcher in history, but a craftsman whose innovations in the use of plate tone and the integration of diverse techniques on a single copper plate had a profound impact on the history of printmaking. The artist's earliest painting dates to 1625 (*The Stoning of St. Stephen*, Lyon, Musée des Beaux-Arts), and his earliest dated prints (see cat. no. 1) were executed in 1628. He continued producing prints, well over two hundred, until 1665, within four years of his death. Thus Rembrandt's entire stylistic development is represented in etchings.

His earliest prints are executed in the highly dramatic, Baroque style of the 1620s and early 1630s (e.g. cat. nos. 25–30), heavily influenced by his early master Pieter Lastman, by the Dutch Caravaggists, and by Antonio Tempesta and Jacques Callot. The gradual moderation of that style is reflected in his work after his permanent move to Amsterdam late in 1631. There he was influenced by prints after Rubens and the works of Annibale Carracci, but also by his exposure more generally to the history of art and his acquaintance with Amsterdam's leading literary, intellectual, and social figures of the time, the last thanks to the connections of his beloved wife Saskia. Rembrandt's prints during this period evince his rapid technical mastery of the possibilities of etching, further liberating his stylistic expression.

The 1640s and early 1650s constitute a period of transition marked by the personal dramas of the death of Saskia, his increasing financial problems, the breach-of-promise suit of Geertge Dircx, and his relationship with Hendrickje Stoffels. During this period, while still experimenting with the dramatic effects of light, as in *The Three Trees* (cat. no. 67), he also was influenced by the art of Mantegna, Leonardo, Raphael, and the Venetian school to seek a greater harmony and classical balance in his compositions (e.g. cat. nos. 55–58, 68, 79). It was during this period that the artist executed all 27 of his landscape prints. Working commonly within a narrower range of light contrast, he increasingly eschewed powerful physical drama for closer examination of the internal, spiritual dimension of the individual at moments of personal crisis (e.g. cat. nos. 20, 21, 39, 54, 55, 58). His works during his last decade of printmaking are characterized by an even greater immersion in the subtleties of the human psyche

and by a deeper study of the art of the Italian Renaissance (cat. nos. 24, 41, 42, 63). During this period he created subtle modulations of tone through an extraordinary mastery of the technical possibilities of printmaking.

A consummate draftsman, Rembrandt commonly drew in reed pen and ink. It is no wonder that etching, the process of drawing with the etching needle through resin onto a copper plate, appealed to him as a natural means of personal expression. Virtually all of Rembrandt's prints were executed as independent works of art; fewer than ten served as book illustrations. As is evident from the multiple states of many of his etchings, printmaking clearly permitted the artist to explore compositional possibilities, to examine figure types, and to build his repertoire of human imagery. (The role of printmaking in his self-portraits is discussed with cat. no. 4.) The medium also enabled him to convey visual effects and moods impossible to attain in painting, and to work with an immediacy and spontaneity comparable in effect to drawing, yet resulting in images that could be reproduced.

The catalogue is organized chronologically by genre. With occasional exceptions, within each genre the sequence corresponds to the numbering in Arthur Hind's 1923 catalogue raisonné. For titles and states, however, we have relied on the authoritative modern catalogue of the illustrated Hollstein, compiled by Christopher White and Karel G. Boon, published in 1969. Both catalogue numbers are indicated with each entry, the former by "H.," the latter by "B. [Bartsch, 1797], Holl." Height always precedes width in stated dimensions. We also have provided concordances of the two catalogue raisonné numbering systems, the Weil catalogue entry numbers, and the titles of the prints. Publication data for these works and other catalogues raisonnés and works cited in the entries are provided in the Bibliography of Works Cited.

As the Bibliography indicates, my entries draw on the research of many recent and not-so-recent scholars in the field. Rembrandt scholarship is so rich that it seemed pointless to include any summary biographical essay on the artist; we offer instead a chronological table of the high points of the artist's life and career. For an introductory study, the reader is encouraged to consult three books, all listed in the Bibliography. Jakob Rosenberg's *Rembrandt: Life and Work*, first published in 1948, remains one of the finest examples of inspired, passionate, and scholarly art historical writing, based on a lifetime of research and devotion by one of the greatest Rembrandt scholars of all time. Christopher White's *Rembrandt and His World*, first published in 1964 and substantially revised in 1984, is a highly readable and informative introduction to the artist's life and career; and the same author's scholarly and insightful *Rembrandt as an Etcher*, published in 1969, is the finest modern study of the technical evolution of the artist's prints.

Adolph Weil's sensibility as a collector and his love for

his prints place him within a tradition of great *amateurs collectionneurs* of the past. It is appropriate, therefore, that his prints bear provenances of such esteemed collectors as Mariette, Hibbert, Danby Seymour, Robert-Dumesnil, Rechberger, Davidsohn, Downe, Nowell-Usticke, and Somary. That these prints, now expressing a single collector's vision, can be appreciated by so many people is both exciting and joyful. To quote Proust:

Through art alone are we able to emerge from ourselves, to know what another person sees of a universe which is not the same as our own and of which, without art, the landscapes would remain as unknown to us as those that may exist in the moon. Thanks to art, instead of seeing one world only, our own, we see that world multiply itself and we have at our disposal as many worlds as there are original artists, . . . worlds which, centuries after the extinction of the fire from which their light first emanated, be that fire called Rembrandt or Vermeer, send us still each one its special radiance.

HILLIARD T. GOLDFARB
Curator for European Art

An Interview with Adolph Weil, Jr.

Friday, December 19, 1986

H G : The first question is obvious: How did you become attracted to the work of Rembrandt?

A W : Well, part of it was, I was influenced by my mother. He was her favorite artist. She thought he was a great colorist, and, having seen some Rembrandt paintings, I did not understand until much later what she meant by that. I'd always thought of color as something very, very vivid—like the Benton in the hall—very vivid colors. I didn't understand, because Rembrandt's painting of colors is not always vivid, they can be very subtle. And the way he used them . . . it's not the kind of color that you see in an Andrea del Sarto or Raphael or Titian—it's much more subtle. And I think he was a great colorist in that sense.

But I think mostly my mother was attracted to Rembrandt by his humanitarian interest in character. And when I first started collecting, of the three printmakers that I chose to collect—Rembrandt, Whistler, and Dürer—of the three, I came to like Rembrandt the most.

H G : How did you first become interested in prints?

A W : When I was a boy, my father, who traveled to Europe every summer to sell cotton to mills in France, Italy, Germany, England, and so forth, would take my mother and my sisters and brother and me to Europe with him. While he was visiting mills, mother would take us to museums or even on tours with a lady from Montgomery who gave very sophisticated tours aimed mostly at art and architecture. I became very much interested in art and wanted to collect, but realized that when I became of age I could hardly afford to buy expensive art, so I started to buy prints.

H G : Do you remember the very first print you ever purchased?

A W : Yes, I do. It was a lithograph by Pissarro, named *La Charrue*, and I still have it. It's a color lithograph, and very elaborate.

H G : Do you remember the first Rembrandt?

A W : I think the first Rembrandt I bought—if my memory serves me right—was from Colnaghi in London in 1971. It was an etching of his mother, Hind number one, you know. I asked Mr. Driver, who was then in charge, if he had something that I could afford, and he brought this print out and showed it to me, and I bought it.

H G : Do you remember why you were attracted—just out of curiosity—to that Pissarro first?

A W : Well, my wife Jean and I were walking down Madison Avenue, I guess, and we passed this gallery. We saw some paintings and prints in the window, and went inside. At first I was attracted to *Le Chapeau Epinglé* by Renoir, but when I saw *La Charrue*, I decided to buy *La Charrue*, and Jean agreed.

H G : When did you first start thinking of yourself as a print collector?

A W : I don't think there is an answer to that. It was a gradual thing. The first prints I bought as a group, because I was afraid to go into the old masters, were Whistlers, for the most part.

H G : In a way, though, he really is a great old master, too, isn't he?

A W : Well, I think so, too, but at the time he wasn't priced that high.

H G : So which printmakers have you specifically pursued since then? Which ones have come to appeal to you especially? Dürer, Rembrandt . . . ?

A W : Dürer, Rembrandt, Whistler, Canaletto, Giovanni Battista Tiepolo, Blake, Goya, Lucas van Leyden, . . . I like Schongauer, but I bought only one. Because I didn't think that I should have just one in my collection, finding his good ones very expensive, I decided to give that one to a museum.

H G : Getting back to Rembrandt, what do you find first attracts you to his prints—the subject matter, the quality of the impression, or a combination of factors?

A W : The subject matter, I think, more than anything else. But on a cruise once, I met a man by the name of Lee

Kolker who was an outstanding collector. I asked him about collecting. He gave me two pieces of advice which were very good, and which I think are still very good. He said, in the first place, don't try to collect everything, just limit yourself to a very few artists whom you prefer. And second, always try to buy quality, because if you buy a print that's in terrible condition or poorly done, you tire of it all too quickly; but when you buy quality, it stays with you.

H G: Very true. What, to you, are the greatest prints of Rembrandt, and what are your favorite subjects, because these may not be the same?

A W: Well, I think the greatest prints, and I don't have any of them, are *The Three Crosses, Christ Presented to the People,* and also *The Hundred Guilder Print,* which I think is gorgeous. My favorites are *Abraham's Sacrifice, The Great Jewish Bride,* and *The Three Trees.*

H G: What is your most pleasant experience or memory associated with acquiring prints, and were there any that were unpleasant or surprising?

A W: All my experiences, that I can remember, were pleasant, and in collecting I've used some very good galleries, like Colnaghi and Schab and Tunick, Linda Papaharis, Kennedy when Alvin Rees was there. But I also have learned to depend very much on Mark Rosen, in Sotheby's Sales—he's been very helpful.

H G: You anticipated my next question: you have bought from both dealers and auctions. Which have you generally found more rewarding?

A W: Both. Occasionally I have been awfully lucky buying at auctions. For instance, when I bought a Mantegna at Karl and Faber, I couldn't read German. So I just bid for it—*The Battle of the Sea Gods.* And when it came in, I was disappointed, because it had been cut within the platemark. I found out later that, with a Mantegna, that doesn't make the difference it would with a later artist.

You mentioned a pleasant experience and a peculiar experience: Kornfeld and Klipstein had two catalogues at the same time—one was the old master catalogue, and the other was the modern master catalogue. I thought I was bidding on a Rembrandt, in the old master catalogue, and I put the wrong number down. I actually bid for something in the modern catalogue, which turned out to be two impressions from different states of an etching by Pissarro, which I later gave to the Boston Museum of Fine Arts. I was very much surprised and somewhat disappointed, because I'd wanted the Rembrandt. But it was a nice etching by Pissarro. (*Chuckle*)

H G: Obviously your Rembrandt collection has grown far beyond your original expectations. Do you have any visions of it now? I mean, do you have an overall view of what you'd like the collection to be, or are you proceeding on a print-by-print basis?

A W: A print-by-print basis. There are some prints by Rembrandt that I really don't like. I don't like the subject matter. There are some that I would love, like the three that I mentioned in the beginning as being what I thought

were the greatest. But they've gotten to be out of reach, if you're trying to buy quality.

H G: Your print collection includes works by a broad range of old masters: Mantegna, Dürer, Lucas, Canaletto, Ribera, Tiepolo; also Goya, Callot, Kerr Eby, Benton, and others. Do you have any guiding principles for your choice of artists and prints, beyond what you've said so far? Can you see yourself expanding in other sorts of directions?

A W: Well, . . . I don't think so anymore. I'm still trying to buy the prints I'm missing from the *Scherzi* by Tiepolo, but I haven't found them at all, in galleries or in auctions. I have all of the prints of Canaletto that one can buy, though I might have one that I ought to upgrade. I don't think I'll broaden out to other artists, unless I see something that absolutely thrills me.

H G: So, the ultimate parameters of your collection indeed reflect the guidelines that the gentleman recommended to you on the cruise: not to have every Rembrandt, or a comprehensive collection, not that sort of American collector's approach, but rather to have individual prints of quality, a more Central European vision of collecting.

A W: That's right, exactly.

H G: We've been talking about prints almost exclusively, but you also own a very choice group of French Impressionists and American nineteenth- and twentieth-century oil paintings, pastels, watercolors, and several outstanding bronzes. How do you regard your print collection in relationship to your other works of art?

A W: Well, the other works of which you are speaking are not owned by me; they are owned by my brother and myself. We acquired them in a very eccentric way, I guess. We would see something come up for sale, or at auctions; then I would like it, and he would like it, and we would decide together whether we should go ahead and try to buy it, and we did. So, we both loved Impressionist paintings, and I guess that's how we bought them. We both loved Winslow Homer, Rodin, and we liked artists like Hopper and Toulouse-Lautrec.

H G: In retrospect, it must be gratifying to realize that you showed such foresight. Now that the market has become so impossible, you have these works that you love, works that you were able to get because you pursued them earlier.

A W: Yes. My father and my uncle, when they occupied the office that my brother and I now occupy, had steel desks. They were very Spartan; everything was business. My brother and I decided we'd try to live in an office that was more homelike, and this is when we started buying paintings, and rugs, antique furniture, and the like.

H G: That leads me to the next question: What is the gratification, for you, in collecting?

A W: Well, I think any work of art that you come to like becomes like a friend. I mean . . . the gratification comes from looking at something, and sometimes seeing something that you never saw before in a painting or a work of art. But I guess everybody who collects anything is on an ego trip to some degree . . .

H G: But it also seems to fulfill a need—not only of ego, but an emotional need.

A W: Yes.

H G: Finally, I want to ask you a couple of questions about Dartmouth and the exhibition. You've mentioned Churchill Lathrop to me. Why does he stand out in your memories of Dartmouth?

A W: Why? Well, because I think that after those trips to Europe that I made with my parents, and going through the great museums in Europe without knowing anything about the history of a relationship of one artist to another, Jerry brought all of that together in the courses I took from him. And I got a greater understanding of what I had seen from his courses. And he was an extremely interesting lecturer, very stimulating. I also should say that Professor Stearns, who probably is forgotten now—in his course we studied Greek and Roman sculpture, and I remember how inspiring that was to me. I still think that the classic period of Greek sculpture, the paintings of the Renaissance, the printmaking of the Renaissance, the painting of the Impressionists . . . along with the founding of our country, and the Declaration of Independence, and the Constitution . . . these were periods of great, great genius. So many geniuses came together and practiced all at the same time, and this has always been a wonder to me.

H G: Has the preparation of the exhibition itself affected your own view of your Rembrandt collection?

A W: I think it's been extremely interesting and helpful to me. For instance, when you compare the first and second state of the *Jan Lutma* . . . the way that Rembrandt built character in the second state . . .

H G: What are your expectations and hopes for the exhibition itself?

A W: What I really hope for is that students in the art department and also students generally will find an interest in it.

H G: Finally, what was the first print that really moved you? Do you remember? Because often prints are a medium that you come to through an experience, by one print really pulling you in.

A W: I think that the one that I can remember best was before the cruise when I met Lee Kolker. I was in New York and I went into the Kennedy Gallery. Alvin Rees was there, and I was admiring a *Saint Jerome* by Dürer on the wall. And I said, oh gosh, isn't that just simply fabulous. And Mr. Rees overheard me, and he said if you think that's great, let me show you something. And he went in back and brought out the Dürer *Saint Jerome* that I bought. It was by far the most expensive print I'd ever bought until that time. It overwhelmed me, that particular print. It is a gorgeous print. Most of the time when I've bought prints, I've been attracted to the ones I've bought, whether a *Saint Jerome* by Ribera, or a *Saint Jerome* by Dürer, or a *Saint Jerome* by Rembrandt.

Portraits

1 The Artist's Mother, Head and Bust: Three Quarters Right

Date of execution: 1628
Definitive catalogues: H. 1; B., Holl. 354, state II/II
Process: etching and drypoint
Data on plate: upper right corner: RHL (monogram) 1628 (2 reversed)
Data on print: on verso, lower right corner: c. 37748 (pencil)
Dimensions: 66 mm x 64 mm (2⅝" x 2⁹⁄₁₆") platemark
        71 mm x 67 mm (2¹³⁄₁₆" x 2⅝") sheet
Watermarks: –
Collections: (Colnaghi's, London, July 9, 1971)

Neeltgen Willemsdochter van Zuybroek, a baker's daughter, gave birth to Rembrandt, the eighth of nine children, in 1606. Rembrandt appears to have been very attached to his mother; she is the subject of six of his etchings, including his first two (this one and B., Holl. 352). She also appears in a wide range of Biblical subjects painted or etched between 1628 and 1633. These etched portrait studies thus provided Rembrandt with the means to explore and develop a repertoire of figure types, drawn from his intimate experience, to be applied to religious and historical themes. It is not surprising that the young artist, who so often portrayed his own face in an effort to understand facial types and expressions, should have turned to his mother as a subject. Although there is no documentary proof that the subject is his mother, in the 1679 inventory of Rembrandt's friend and client Clement de Jonghe (see cat. no. 23) the title "Rembrandt's Mother" is already applied to another portrait etching of 1631 of the same venerable subject (B., Holl. 343).

Among Rembrandt's earliest etchings, this dated work of 1628 is also a print of great rarity, here exhibited in a fine impression pulled early in the second state. Touches of drypoint are visible throughout, notably in the sleeve, the veil, and the ruff and over the subject's left eye. In the first state Rembrandt modeled the face and head of his subject with great specificity, only preliminarily indicating her torso in a few extended, faint strokes. In the second state the drapery was added, together with the veil that bridges the separately studied elements and the flickering drypoint, which so effectively unifies the visual impression of the figure in a tactilely evocative manner. It is very rare that one finds as much drypoint in this print as appears in this impression.

Even at the outset of his graphic career Rembrandt reveals his sensitivity to the complementary use of etching and drypoint and to the luminous potential of the paper itself. One of the great draftsmen of all time, Rembrandt uses the etching needle much like a pen, drawing through the resin-coated plate in rapid yet delicate strokes.

2 Bust of a Man Wearing a High Cap, Three Quarters Right: The Artist's Father (?)

Date of execution: 1630
Definitive catalogues: H. 22; B., Holl. 321, state I/II
Process: etching
Data on plate: upper left corner: RHL (monogram) 1630
Data on print: The print is mounted. On verso of backing paper, lower center: B321 (pencil)
Dimensions: 105 mm x 89 mm (4⅛″ x 3½″) trimmed just within platemark on all sides
Watermarks: mounted
Collections: (Sotheby's, London, June 26, 1986, lot 709)

While there is a relative consensus concerning the identification of Rembrandt's mother, the name of his father, who was buried on April 27, 1630, has been assigned to a variety of elderly male subjects. Among Rembrandt's contemporary portrait drawings of elderly bearded men, one bearing a non-autograph seventeenth-century inscription identifying the subject as Rembrandt's father exists at Oxford, Ashmolean Museum (Benesch 56), but the sitter is not the same as the one in this print. Between 1630 and 1631 Rembrandt executed a series of etchings, drawings, and paintings of elderly men. The present print closely resembles a painting of an *Elderly Man in a High Cap* in the Tiroler Landesmuseum Ferdinandeum at Innsbruck.

As with the images of his mother, the portraits of elderly men served Rembrandt as characterful types to be drawn from for his religious paintings. Both in his early career and in his late works, he seems to have been particularly fascinated by the subtle, complex, and profound records of experience and suffering conveyed in the faces of the elderly.

This is a very good impression of the rare first state of this print, before the plate was reduced. The artist has left a film of ink on the surface of the etching plate (plate tone), which is particularly evident in the wiping strokes across the chest of the figure. The print has been trimmed somewhat irregularly just within the platemark all around, there are some minor visible defects in condition, and a touch of India ink was applied at a later date to the nose.

3 Bald Headed Man in Profile Right; The Artist's Father (?)

Date of execution: 1630

Definitive catalogues: H. 23; B., Holl. 292, state III/III

Process: etching

Data on plate: lower right: RHL (monogram) 1630

Data on print: on verso, upper center: 153 (pencil); upper right: 3000 (pencil); left center, vertically: 14757 (pencil); lower left center: 292iv (pencil); 23 (pencil, over erased B292); lower right corner: vs (pencil).

Dimensions: 69 mm x 58 mm (2¹¹⁄₁₆″ x 2¼″) platemark
    70 mm x 59 mm (2¾″ x 2⁵⁄₁₆″) sheet

Watermarks: –

Collections: on verso, lower right center: F. F. Hansen (pencil) and Lugt 2813 [F. F. Hansen, Copenhagen, 1823–1916]; C. G. Boerner auction LXX (1911), lot 533; Gordon Nowell-Usticke (Sotheby Parke Bernet, New York, October 31, 1967, lot 41); (W. H. Schab, December 6, 1984)

This etching is another of the group of over a dozen portrait studies of elderly men that Rembrandt etched between 1630 and the autumn of 1631, when he left Leyden to establish himself permanently at Amsterdam. Several of these portraits have been traditionally associated with Rembrandt's father (see cat. no. 2). This impression is an unusually brilliant one in which the glistening ink surface is of a remarkable, rarely seen freshness.

As in the 1628 portrait of his mother (cat. no. 1), Rembrandt began by focusing in the first state exclusively on the head, set on a larger etching plate, presumably anticipating the additions of the second state. In the second state the artist depicted the subject wearing a robe similar to the one in cat. no. 2, and a broad pectoral necklace, the sort of costume and trappings commonly kept in the studio of a historical painter. In the third state, however, the artist has cut down the plate and shadowed in the background to bring the head of the subject into greater focus and relief, more intimately exploring and shading his features and thereby creating a more penetrating psychological study.

4 Self Portrait in a Fur Cap: Bust

Date of execution: 1630

Definitive catalogues: H. 29; B., Holl. 24, state IV/IV

Process: etching

Data on plate: upper left corner: RHL (monogram) 1630

Data on print: on verso, center: s.38647 (pencil); below preceding: s.29-wl(?) .226.D24 (pencil); lower left corner: B. 24 iv (pencil); bottom center: A24 (pencil)

Dimensions: 63 mm x 52 mm (2½″ x 2 1/16″) cut to platemark

Watermarks: –

Collections: on verso, lower left center: Lugt 1802 [N. Mossoloff, Moscow, 1847–1914]; upper center: inventory stamp (blue) of the Museum Roumiantzoff, Moscow, inv. no. 19885; sale of estate of James Kingon Callaghan (Sotheby Parke Bernet, New York, November 14, 1981, lot 815)

Rembrandt's production of self-portraits is without parallel in the history of Western art. Over twenty etchings and sixty paintings he executed of himself survive (most of the etched self-portraits dating between 1628 and 1634), and his face appears in numerous other nonportrait works. Although portraiture provided a steady means of livelihood for a seventeenth-century Dutch artist, especially for Rembrandt, and although, as noted, the artist could serve as a convenient model for studies of character and expression, there certainly must have been some psychological pressure, some need to penetrate his own spiritual life through his artistic eye, behind the production of such a large corpus of works for which there would be minimal commercial demand.

The images are hardly flattering. The early self-portraits tend to fall into two categories: studies of emotional expression and direct, "passive" studies of his own features. In this print the 23-year-old artist presents us with a trenchant, direct, uncompromising image of his face, with its bulbous nose and peering eyes. Although he originally began the etching on a larger plate, evident in the first state, he apparently decided immediately to focus on the face, and he reduced the plate in the second state without ever elaborating the bust. Subsequent changes in state reflect additions in the shading lines. The fur cap, charged with a pen-and-ink effect of rapid, short strokes, shades the artist's brow and serves to frame and emphasize his intent gaze. Rembrandt has printed this impression on a warm, golden-tan paper and has left a thin film of plate tone. Wiping marks appear throughout the sheet.

5 The Artist's Mother Seated, in an Oriental Headdress: Half Length

Date of execution: 1631

Definitive catalogues: H. 51; B., Holl. 348, state II/III

Process: etching

Data on plate: lower right: RHL (monogram) 1631

Data on print: on verso, top center: 3 (pencil); lower left: 343 (pencil); lower left corner: e/e/– (pencil); below preceding: 343 (pencil)

Dimensions: 140 mm x 126 mm (5½" x 4¹⁵⁄₁₆") trimmed within platemark on all sides

Watermarks: –

Collections: on verso, lower left corner: AW (pencil) [Adolph Weil, Jr., Montgomery, Alabama]; below preceding: Lugt 176 [H. Danby Seymour, London and Trent, 1820–1877]; (Sotheby's, London, May 8, 1975, lot 590)

In this print of 1631 Rembrandt approaches the portraiture of his mother with greater formality and monumentality, and also with less intimacy, than in his study of 1628 (cat no. 1). With a new mastery and sureness both of composition and of technique, the artist has worked out the entire composition in the first state, reducing the shadow on the left from above the head to the shoulders in the second state, thereby placing the head in bolder, more sculptural relief in the latter state. Rembrandt also has reworked the sleeve, giving it greater density and richness, and has added the floral pattern that appears on the veil of the headdress. A subsequent so-called third state is actually heavily reworked by another hand.

Figure 1. Rembrandt, *The Artist's Mother Seated at a Table, Looking Right: Three Quarter Length*, etching, state I/III, Amsterdam, Rijksmuseum

6 *Circle of Rembrandt*
The Artist's Mother in Widow's Dress and Black Gloves

Date of execution: c. 1632

Definitive catalogues: H. 91; B., Holl. 344, state I/I

Process: etching and drypoint

Data on plate: upper left: Rembrandt f. [the same signature hand appears in B., Holl. 286–289, autograph prints, but the signature is not autograph]

Data on print: on verso, lower right corner: M:C (pencil)

Dimensions: 149 mm x 116 mm (5⅞″ x 4⁹⁄₁₆″) platemark
157 mm x 124 mm (6³⁄₁₆″ x 4⅞″) sheet

Watermarks: partial foolscap

Collections: on recto, upper left corner: Lugt 2849 [G. Hibbert, London, 1757–1837]; on verso, upper right corner: Lugt 1419 [John Barnard, London, d. 1784]; (Christie's, London, July 15, 1982, lot 422)

The difference in handling of technique and the resulting difference in psychological profundity between a work by the young master and an accomplished effort by a follower is strikingly apparent in this portrait, probably executed by an early pupil of Rembrandt and based on an autograph print (B., Holl. 343, figure 1). The portrait type in both prints is that of a cool, formalized presentation of Rembrandt's mother in her widow's attire (Rembrandt's father had died on April 23, 1630), but the autograph work is infused with a sense of the stern and personalized actuality of the sitter.

In the present print, the artist has carefully attempted to render surfaces but with little sensitivity to inner spiritual life. The etching needle has been used with great energy but without focus, resulting in an ambiguous sense of space and volume. The face is hard and mannequin-like. Although the print appears in early catalogues raisonnés, Jan Six first suggested that the plate was retouched by a Rembrandt pupil ("Gersaints lijst van Rembrandts prenten," *Oud Holland*, XXVII [1909], p. 99). Münz has proposed Ferdinand Bol as the etcher; Christopher White and Karel Boon have suggested Karel van der Pluym.

7 Jan Cornelis Sylvius, Preacher

Date of execution: 1633

Definitive catalogues: H. 111; B., Holl. 266, state I/II

Process: etching

Data on plate: left center: Rembrandt f 1633

Data on print: on recto, in right margin: 247 (pencil); right bottom margin near corner: d (pencil)

Dimensions: 167 mm x 142 mm (6⅝″ x 5⁹⁄₁₆″) platemark
176 mm x 150 mm (6¹⁵⁄₁₆″ x 5¹⁵⁄₁₆″) sheet

Watermarks: foolscap (Heawood 1921)

Collections: on verso, lower left corner: Lugt 719a [Viscount Downe, Wykeham Abbey, Scarborough, b. 1903]; (W. H. Schab, April 6, 1972)

After several country posts and his appointment to the Gasthuiskerk in Amsterdam in 1610, Jan Cornelis Sylvius (1564–1638) was nominated preacher at the Groote Kerk in Amsterdam in 1622. Sylvius was the guardian of the young orphan and heiress Saskia van Uylenburch (twenty years old in 1633), to whom he was related through his wife. That same year, Rembrandt was betrothed to Saskia. In many of his portraits of 1632–33 (over forty such dated paintings alone) Rembrandt presents his subjects against neutral backdrops, the figures dominating the space by their monumentality and clear, powerful stances and gestures. In his portrait of the prominent Reformed Church minister, however, the subject is shown seated before a column in a darkened chamber, dressed solemnly, looking up toward the viewer with great dignity yet with warmth and intimacy of expression. His eyes do not meet ours, as if the preacher's mind were still contemplating the Scriptural passage he had been studying.

Rembrandt has achieved in this print a new mastery in harmonizing the diverse compositional elements. The preacher's simple, sober attire, the cool lighting in which only the Bible and the head of the minister, framed by his ruff, are highlighted, the solemn vaulted interior, the shadowed, stout column complementing the posed, stable, vertical figure of Sylvius, whose folded hands lie calmly and reverently on the Scriptures, all serve to convey the spiritual life and integrity of the subject.

In the second state Rembrandt attempted to define Sylvius's head further by extensively shading and darkening his clothing and the chamber. This resulted, however, in a less sensitive and atmospheric image, and the first state, exhibited here, is generally deemed more successful.

8 Self Portrait with Raised Sabre

Date of execution: 1634

Definitive catalogues: H. 109; B., Holl. 18, state II/II

Process: etching and burin

Data on plate: upper left corner: Rembrandt f. 1634

Data on print: on verso, center: fn (?) 23 (pencil); lower left
    corner: 15 (pencil); bottom center: 18iii B (pencil); below
    preceding: 109 (pencil); lower right corner: NV. (pencil)

Dimensions: 123 mm x 101 mm (4⅞″ x 4″) trimmed to platemark

Watermarks: –

Collections: on verso, upper right: Lugt 1788 (brown ink),
    "P. mariette. 1661" [Pierre Mariette II, Paris, 1634–1716];
    lower left corner: Lugt 407 [B. Randall, Baltimore, 20th c.];
    (Christie's, New York, January 23, 1982, lot 390)

One of the more remarkable self-portraits of Rembrandt's
early maturity in Amsterdam, the *Self Portrait with Raised
Sabre* of 1634 presents the artist in a highly dramatic,
confrontational, frontal pose, wearing oriental attire and
baring a saber. By this date Rembrandt had become a
successful and famous painter in his adopted city. That
same year he married Saskia van Uylenburch, the rich
orphan of a prominent, well-connected family. During
these early Amsterdam years Rembrandt portrayed himself
in both paintings and prints in the sumptuous attire and
ornaments that he collected as props for his studio. In
the highly specialized art market of Amsterdam, Rembrandt succeeded his early master, Pieter Lastman, as the
leading religious and historical painter. The exotic elements
featured in these portraits also appear in his religious
subjects of these years (see cat. no. 46 and cat. no. 54,
figure 17). Yet despite the gorgeous trappings and the
menacing gesture with the sword that so effectively frames
the face and animates the portrait, it is Rembrandt's own
proletarian countenance that dominates the work.

9 Self Portrait with Plumed Cap and Lowered Sabre

Figure 2. Rembrandt, *Self Portrait with Plumed Cap and Lowered Sabre*, etching, state I/III, Amsterdam, Rijksmuseum

Date of execution: 1634

Definitive catalogues: Hind 110; B., Holl. 23, state III/III

Process: etching and burin

Data on plate: lower right, following diagonal of sleeve: Rembrandt f 1634

Data on print: on verso, lower left center: 0–1 (pencil); lower center: fine and rare (pencil); below preceding: 2___28 (pencil); lower left corner: 8G (pencil); below preceding: 4.110 III (pencil); bottom left center: Lls/_/_ (pencil); A21373 (pencil); lower right corner: ISXX (pencil); Col (pencil).

Dimensions: 130 mm x 109 mm (5⅟₁₆″ x 4¼″) platemark
134 mm x 118 mm (5⁵⁄₁₆″ x 4⅝″) sheet

Watermarks: –

Collections: on verso, lower left corner, stamped in black ink: (PMMP); inscribed on mat: ex-collection J. William Middendorf III; (L. Papaharis, October 14, 1983)

The *Self Portrait with Plumed Hat and Lowered Sabre* originally depicted Rembrandt with much the same attire and exotic panache of cat. no. 8, but the artist made important modifications in the second state. In the first state (figure 2) the artist depicts himself at three-quarter length, the saber featured in the previous print supporting his left hand. The etching is a dazzling study of the rich brocades, fabrics, and jewels with which the artist has adorned himself. In the second state, however, he has significantly reduced the print to an irregular-oval bust study, focusing the composition on the sharply lit, unflattering depiction of his visage, shading the background and darkening his drapery so as to project even more aggressively his face with its prominent nose and sharp, squinting eyes. In this brilliant impression of the third state (in which the oval is made regular) it is on the artist himself, with his face and disquieting stare, that the viewer's attention is riveted.

10 The Great Jewish Bride

Date of execution: 1635

Definitive catalogues: H. 127; B., Holl. 340, state V/V

Process: etching, drypoint, and burin

Data on plate: lower left: R 1635 (reversed)

Data on print: on verso, center: 795 (pencil); lower center: W. 330 III (pencil); lower right: 4 (pencil); 199 (upside down) (pencil); bottom left: 1) 1500 (pencil)

Dimensions: 220 mm x 167 mm (8⅝″ x 6⁹⁄₁₆″) trimmed to platemark (just within platemark on right side)

Watermarks: fleur-de-lys, similar to Heawood 1730 and especially to Heawood 1772

Collections: on verso, lower right center: Lugt 1788 (brown ink), "P. mariette 1674" [Pierre Mariette II, Paris, 1634–1716]; lower left corner: Lugt 1383 [Hermann Weber, Bonn, 1817–1854]; (Theodore Donson, December 2, 1981); upper right center: W (pencil) [Adolph Weil, Jr., Montgomery, Alabama]

The traditional title of this print, *The Great Jewish Bride*, was first given to the subject in 1733 by the Delft collector Valerius Röver (1686–1739). Röver's meticulous manuscript inventory of his collection, begun in 1705, is preserved at the library of the University of Amsterdam. (For further information see Lugt suppl. 2984a–c and articles listed in the Bibliography of this catalogue.) His appellation was based on the mistaken belief that the print represented the daughter of Rembrandt's friend Ephraim Bonus (see cat. no. 21; Bonus would have been only 36 in 1635). In the first catalogue raisonné of Rembrandt's prints, that of E.-F. Gersaint (Paris, 1751), the title is repeated. Gersaint notes that the string of pearls and free-falling hair were the coiffure worn by Jewish maidens when they were betrothed in seventeenth-century Holland. This seems to be true, and the scroll the woman holds may be a Jewish wedding contract (*ketuba*).

Other suggestions have included an actress playing the role of Minerva (Valentiner), a classical sibyl (Weisbach, Benesch), and the Biblical Esther preparing to meet King Ahasuerus (Kahr), a subject painted by the artist in 1633 that shows a woman of similar appearance wearing a jeweled hairband, her loosely falling hair being brushed by an attendant (Ottawa, National Gallery of Canada). The document held by the woman in the print, therefore, could be the royal decree against the Jews (Esther 4.15–17).

The traditional interpretation of a Jewish bride becomes less tenable if, as some scholars contend, the features of the young woman are based on those of Saskia (the resemblance is even more evident in the preparatory drawing for the print in the Stockholm Nationalmuseum, Benesch 292). Indeed, Rembrandt's depiction of Saskia as St. Catherine in 1638 (the so-called *Little Jewish Bride*, cat. no. 16) would tend to confirm this identification.

In the first two states of the print Rembrandt worked up only the head and shoulders of the model and the vaulted interior; the torso and the brocaded drapery were drawn and the luminous effects of lighting were created in subsequent states. The present exceedingly rich, darkly inked impression of the fifth state presents the artist's final vision of the subject.

11 Old Woman Sleeping

Date of execution: 1635/37

Definitive catalogues: H. 129; B., Holl. 350, state I/I

Process: etching

Data on plate: –

Data on print: on verso, lower right center: B 350 (pencil); lower right: πmor (diagonally, pencil); bottom left center: 10162 (pencil, with a diagonal pencil line running down from the preceding)

Dimensions: 68 mm x 52 mm (2¹¹⁄₁₆″ x 2¹⁄₁₆″) platemark
71 mm x 54 mm (2¹³⁄₁₆″ x 2⅛″) sheet

Watermarks: –

Collections: A. J. Godby (Lugt 1119b, no stamp, Baltimore and London, 1853–1934); (Sotheby's, London, January 29–30, 1935, lot 248); on verso, lower right corner: Lugt 719a [Viscount Downe, Wykeham Abbey, Scarborough, b. 1903]; (Sotheby's, London, December 7, 1972, lot 221); (Christie's, London, December 6, 1985, lot 331)

The *Old Woman Sleeping* probably represents Rembrandt's mother and is among the small group of images of her executed during his years in Amsterdam. She died in Leyden in September 1640. In his celebrated painting of 1631, Rembrandt had portrayed her as the *Prophetess Anna* (Amsterdam, Rijksmuseum), attired in rich velvets and brocades and studying the Bible, her hand caressing the Scriptures as she reads. In a noteworthy departure from his earlier, more formal or allegorical presentations, the artist depicts in this etching an intimate, quiet moment of no great symbolic meaning, capturing in a single state the dozing of the aged woman, who had been reading. The aesthetic mastery of his technique is evident precisely in intimate details: note the shadows of the eyeglasses and of the bookmark.

Figure 3. Rembrandt, *Self Portrait with Saskia*, Dresden, Staatliche Kunstsammlungen

12 Self Portrait with Saskia

Date of execution: 1636

Definitive catalogues: H. 144; B., Holl. 19, state I/III

Process: etching

Data on plate: upper left corner: Rembrandt.f. 1636

Data on print: on verso, lower right corner: FNO (pencil); (inscriptions and collection mark [?] lower left verso obscured by hinging)

Dimensions: 105 mm x 94 mm (4⅛″ x 3¹¹⁄₁₆″) platemark (trimmed to platemark on left)
108 mm x 95 mm (4¼″ x 3¾″) sheet

Watermarks: mounted

Collections: (see comments above); (Sotheby Parke Bernet, New York, November 14, 1975, lot 88)

Rembrandt clearly adored his wife and depicted her often in paintings, drawings, and prints in a variety of genres. Probably the most famous (if not the most tasteful) of these images is the swaggering double portrait with Saskia seated on his lap and her head turned toward the viewer, himself depicted as the prodigal son toasting with a flute of wine (Dresden, Staatliche Kunstsammlungen, 1635, figure 3). Compared with that dramatic, Baroque composition of "the good life," the *Self Portrait with Saskia* is a sober, more natural and intimate presentation of the married couple. Rembrandt, holding a reed pen (or etching needle), is the dominant figure. He apparently is being shown at work, staring into a mirror and copying his wife's features in reverse (the printing process would reverse the image again).

The first state of this print is particularly desirable. The second and third states, which contain minor corrections to the plate, are marked by a weakening of the features that distinguish fine, early impressions of the first state, of which this is an outstanding example. Note the fine, unusually deep shading under the brim of Rembrandt's hat. Indeed, the entire figure of the artist is more richly inked so that his figure bodes forth in the right foreground while that of Saskia, whose eyes focus on him from the left background—a clever psychological and compositional device—sits half-defined in the unlimited space behind him. Once again, as in his early self-portraits, Rembrandt has set his eyes in shadow to draw us psychologically into the composition as we peer back at him.

13 Samuel Manasseh ben Israel

Date of execution: 1636

Definitive catalogues: H. 146; B., Holl. 269, state III/III

Process: etching

Data on plate: right center: Rembrandt f 1636

Data on print: on verso, upper left corner: (indecipherable, pencil); center: (M) (pencil); lower center: B 269 – II (pencil); below preceding: 602/8 (pencil); below preceding: 8223 (pencil)

Dimensions: 149 mm x 107 mm (5¹³⁄₁₆″ x 4¼″) platemark
151 mm x 110 mm (5¹⁵⁄₁₆″ x 4⁵⁄₁₆″) sheet

Watermarks: partial *M* or *W* (?)

Collections: on recto, bottom center: Lugt 2200 (dry) [A. P. F. Robert-Dumesnil, Paris, 1778–1864]; on verso, bottom center: Lugt 686 [Hamburg, Kunsthalle, duplicate stamp]; below preceding: Lugt 1328 [Hamburg, Kunsthalle]; (Sotheby Parke Bernet, New York, May 8, 1975, lot 583); lower left corner: AW (pencil) [Adolph Weil, Jr., Montgomery, Alabama]

Samuel Manasseh ben Israel was one of the most distinguished members of the Jewish community in Amsterdam. Born in Lisbon in 1604, he immigrated with his family to Amsterdam while still a child. An intellectual prodigy, by the age of eighteen he had already been nominated rabbi of the Portuguese community in his adopted city. He lived on the same street as Rembrandt, and their friendship was both profound and long-lasting. Twenty years later Rembrandt illustrated one of Manasseh ben Israel's works, *Piedra gloriosa de la estatua de Nabuchadnesar,* and we know that the rabbi supplied Rembrandt with various texts and Hebrew manuscripts that appear in his paintings. Manasseh ben Israel died in 1657 during his return from a mission to Oliver Cromwell to secure the readmission of Jews to England.

It has often been noted that in this print Rembrandt demonstrates a new freedom of draftsmanship in his etching technique, applying with mastery to the etching plate the rapid strokes and open hatching that one associates with his contemporary reed-pen-and-ink drawings. The artist has eschewed rich costumes and iconographic paraphernalia in order to focus sympathetically on the calm, intelligent gaze of the subject. The figure is presented with sober directness and simplicity.

14 Bearded Man in a Velvet Cap with a Jewel Clasp

Date of execution: 1637

Definitive catalogues: H. 150; B., Holl. 313, state I/I

Process: etching

Data on plate: upper left corner: Rembrandt f. 1637

Data on print: on verso, center: G_(?)915 (pencil); lower right: B.313/H.150}only state (pencil)

Dimensions: 96 mm x 83 mm (3¾″ x 3¼″) platemark
97 mm x 84 mm (3¹³⁄₁₆″ x 3⁵⁄₁₆″) sheet

Watermarks: –

Collections: on verso, lower right: Lugt 719a [Viscount Downe, Wykeham Abbey, Scarborough, b. 1903]; (Sotheby's, London, December 7, 1972, lot 205); (Sotheby Parke Bernet, New York, November 14, 1981, lot 871)

When this etching of 1637 is compared with Rembrandt's early studies of old men (cat. nos. 2, 3) or his early paintings of old men in oriental garb (e.g. New York, Metropolitan Museum, 1632; Munich, Alte Pinakothek, 1633), the artist's deeper concern with the expression of an individualized personality is all the more striking. In this clear, sharp impression, Rembrandt's masterly use of the medium through an extraordinary range of strokes, from broad contours to rapid scribbles to tiny flecks of the etching needle, is evident in such detail as the sitter's beard, his cape, and the subtle definition of his face.

15 Young Man in a Velvet Cap
(Ferdinand Bol?)

Date of execution: 1637

Definitive catalogues: H. 151; B., Holl. 268, state II/II

Process: etching (touches of gray ink applied)

Data on plate: upper left corner: Rembrandt f 1637

Data on print: on verso, lower left corner: 268 (pencil); lower right corner: 345 (pencil)

Dimensions: 97 mm x 83 mm (3¹³⁄₁₆″ x 3¼″) platemark
          99 mm x 86 mm (3⅞″ x 3⅜″) sheet

Watermarks:–

Collections: on verso, lower right corner: Lugt 567 [d'Arenberg Collection, Brussels and Nordkirchen]; (Kennedy Gallery, New York); (L. Papaharis, March 1983)

The possibility that this portrait might represent the Dutch artist Ferdinand Bol, an early pupil of Rembrandt, was first suggested by F. Schmidt-Degener in 1932. There is a resemblance between the sitter and a so-called self-portrait by Bol in the collection of the Duke of Newcastle, as Christopher White has noted. The print attracted the attention of Degas, who executed both a sketch and a print after this etching.

16 The Little Jewish Bride (Saskia as Saint Catherine)

Date of execution: 1638

Definitive catalogues: H. 154; B., Holl. 342, state I/I

Process: etching and drypoint

Data on plate: upper right corner: Rembrandt f. 1638 (reversed)

Data on print: on verso, upper left corner: D.M 312 (pencil); lower left corner: 11.55 (pencil); lower right center: very fine (pencil, in same hand as "W. Stewart's Collection" [see below])

Dimensions: 110 mm x 78 mm (4⁵⁄₁₆″ x 3¹⁄₁₆″) platemark
114 mm x 84 mm (4½″ x 3⁵⁄₁₆″) sheet

Watermarks: –

Collections: on verso, lower right center: W. (Mr.?) Stewart's Collection (pencil); (Gilhofer and Rauschburg, August 7, 1936); bottom left center: purple collection stamp of Felix Somary (Vienna and Zurich, 1881–1956); (N. G. Stogdon, Somary Sale cat. no. 45, November 14, 1985)

Although traditionally mistitled *The Little Jewish Bride*, the print depicts Saskia in the guise of St. Catherine (note the toothed wheel to her left, the instrument of martyrdom and symbol of the saint). In comparison with *The Great Jewish Bride* (cat. no. 10), for which she had modeled four years earlier, Saskia is posed in this print with great simplicity in one of the most delicate and personal portrayals Rembrandt executed of his wife. In this brilliant impression, which comes from the great Somary collection, the black, clear contours are complemented by extraordinary, vibrant touches of drypoint beneath her hands, underneath her left sleeve, at the base of her neck, and in her hairband. Again, as in the *Samuel Manasseh ben Israel* (cat. no. 13) but with even greater concision, Rembrandt draws on the etching plate with tremendous freedom and a daunting range of strokes. Yet, rather than drawing attention to his technique, with great restraint he presents a touchingly simple and direct image of Saskia.

17 Old Man with a Divided Fur Cap

Date of execution: 1640

Definitive catalogues: H. 170; B., Holl. 265, state I/II

Process: etching and drypoint

Data on plate: upper left corner: Rembrandt f 1640

Data on print: on verso, lower left center: 33195 (pencil); lower left corner: 19303 (pencil); lower right: 87 (pencil); bottom center: B.265/I vor d. Schuldige   Auct. Goldschmidt. Frankfort 1917 (pencil); lower right: (83) (pencil)

Dimensions: 149 mm x 134 mm (5¹³⁄₁₆″ x 5¼″) platemark
181 mm x 163 mm (7⅛″ x 6⁷⁄₁₆″) sheet

Watermarks: AV

Collections: on verso, lower left corner: Lugt 2926 [Rud. Ph. Goldschmidt, Berlin, c.1840–1914]; upper right center: Lugt 1681ter [F. A. Lieberg, Buenos Aires, b. 1898]; (Kornfeld und Klipstein, Bern, auction 170, 1979, lot 97); (R. E. Lewis, February 19, 1986)

This subject appears to have served as a model for several Biblical works by Rembrandt dating from the late 1630s through the mid-1640s, including *Abraham Caressing Isaac* (cat. no. 49, 1637) and *The Triumph of Mordecai* (cat. no. 51, 1641). In this fine impression on a warm, golden-toned paper, the drypoint highlights on the sleeves and buckle are unusually pronounced. Again Rembrandt defines the drapery with the summary mastery of a pen-and-ink sketch.

18 Portrait of a Boy, in Profile

Date of execution: 1641

Definitive catalogues: H. 188; B., Holl. 310, state I/I

Process: etching

Data on plate: upper left corner: Rembrandt f 1641

Data on print: on verso, lower center: 11.311 (pencil); below
   preceding: 311 (partially obscured, pencil); lower left center:
   1 2 2 . 0 (pencil)

Dimensions: 94 mm x 67 mm (3¹¹⁄₁₆″ x 2⅝″) platemark
   95 mm x 68 mm (3¾″ x 2¹¹⁄₁₆″) sheet

Watermarks: –

Collections: on verso, lower left corner: Lugt 58 [Earl of
   Aylesford, London and Packington Hall, Warwickshire,
   1786–1859]; Lugt 1373 [H. S. Olivier, Potterne Manor,
   Wiltshire, 1796–1866]; Lugt 1475 [J. H. Wrenn, Chicago,
   1841–1911]; Lugt 133 [A. Hirsch, Paris, 1843–1884]; (Sotheby
   Parke Bernet, New York, November 14, 1981, lot 868)

The youthful subject of this print has been identified
as Prince William II of Orange, fifteen years old in 1641.
The prince succeeded his father, Frederick-Henry, as
Stathouder of Holland in 1647, but died in 1650 at the age
of twenty-four. Child portraits are rare in Rembrandt's
corpus. Outside of his representations of his son Titus,
there are only seven, and only this single etching. The
youth is presented very formally in profile, a pose rarely
found in Rembrandt after the early 1630s. The social
station of the subject was certainly a consideration in
selecting the pose. The increasing influence of Rembrandt's
study of Renaissance art, both Germanic (Cranach and
Beham) and Italian (Piero della Francesca), has been
cited by Sophie de Bussierre as another influence on the
composition.

The exhibited impression is a fine, particularly early
one, noteworthy for its tonality, with much evident grain
and craquelure. These effects, probably due to cracks in
the varnish/resin and to application of a sulfur tint that
would bite into the plate, were used to sublime effect in his
contemporary landscape *The Windmill* (cat. no. 66).
Christopher White has argued that the effect is due to
uneven burnishing of the copper plate rather than to the
laying on of a sulfur tint; however, the controlled variation
and small corrosive dotting of the plate strongly suggest
the intentional, controlled effect of a sulfur-bitten tone.

Date of execution: 1641

Definitive catalogues: H. 189; B., Holl. 261, state II/IV

Process: etching and drypoint

Data on plate: in apron: Rembrandt f 1641

Data on print: on verso, top center: 6 (brown ink); 50 (pencil); center: 65 (pencil); right center: 6.1 (upside down, brown ink); running down the right edge below preceding: 1412 (red ink); lower right corner: dir- (pencil); along the left edge running up the sheet vertically: NY110-b-b Ger No241 de 2 de mar / 20 (pencil); lower left: B261 (pencil); lower left corner: 3300 S (pencil)

Dimensions: 154 mm x 103 mm (6$\frac{1}{16}$" x 4$\frac{1}{16}$") platemark
158 mm x 107 mm (6$\frac{3}{16}$" x 4$\frac{3}{16}$") sheet

Watermarks: cockatrice with house over initials RP, Heusler of Basle, Churchill 286

Collections: on verso, lower left: Lugt 633b (stamped twice: once black, once blue) [Charles J. Rosenbloom, Pittsburgh, b. 1899]; (Christie's, New York, November 16, 1982, lot 67)

This informal portrait of an unknown model (he appears the same year as the model for *The Cardplayer*, B., Holl. 136) provided the opportunity for Rembrandt to experiment extensively with the use of drypoint. Up to this point in portraiture drypoint had been used by the artist minimally as an accessory to highlight surfaces and enhance textures. The subject is dressed in sixteenth-century attire in a pose which, as Christopher White has noted, is not unlike that of Dürer's *Erasmus*.

As the sketch lines in the apron about Rembrandt's signature indicate, the artist originally conceived of the composition as extending below its present margin. In the second state, here illustrated, he added the effective collar, which sets off the head, and extensive drypoint in the sitter's sleeve and the background, placing the figure within a richly shadowed interior. In the third state, the artist further strengthened the face and hair and darkened the background with additional drypoint. Rembrandt intentionally exposed the face to the acid bath for a shorter period than the rest of the plate, creating the delicate, silvery lighting and sensitive facial definition so evident against the velvety richness of the rest of the plate.

20 Jan Cornelis Sylvius, Preacher

Date of execution: 1646

Definitive catalogues: H. 225; B., Holl. 280, state II/II

Process: etching, drypoint, and burin

Data on plate: upper center: Rembrandt 1646; Latin texts
along edge of oval frame and in apron (see comments below)

Data on print: on verso, lower center: R (pencil); lower left
corner: c6480 (pencil)

Dimensions: 278 mm x 188 mm (10¹⁵⁄₁₆″ x 7⅜″) platemark
283 mm x 192 mm (11⅛″ x 7⁹⁄₁₆″) sheet

Watermarks: coat of arms with Strasburg Bend and Lily and
pendant WK (WR?), similar to Heawood 141

Collections: on verso, lower left corner: Lugt 144 [Alfred
Morrison (?), London and Fonthill, 1821–1897]; (Christie's,
New York, November 16, 1982, lot 70)

Figure 4. Rembrandt, *Posthumous Portrait of Jan Cornelis Sylvius,* pen and brown ink and wash and white gouache, London, British Museum

Jan Cornelis Sylvius died in 1638, but it was in 1646, four years after Saskia's death, at which time he had temporarily abandoned portraiture, that Rembrandt returned to the genre to execute the famous posthumous portrait and homage to her guardian and the minister who had baptized two of their children. This was thirteen years after his previous, less dramatic portrait of the preacher (cat. no. 7). Rembrandt's intention was to illustrate that in the most profound sense the minister still lived, and to achieve this he relied on text, composition, and technique. The Latin text about the symbolic stone frame through which Sylvius's hand reaches out in exhortation to us notes his professional positions, their tenures, and the date of his death. In the apron a Latin ode by the Dutch humanist C. Barleus describes the minister as a man of piety and faith, who loved honesty and simplicity and whose eloquent Christian teachings illuminated the path to God's light and to the stars.

The composition itself, far more vital than that of the 1633 print, is most striking. The idea of a porthole frame for a posthumous portrait may have come to Rembrandt from ex-votos found on seventeenth-century church walls. The idea of a sitter reaching out from within an oval frame already had been realized in paintings by Gerrit Pietersz. (1606) and Frans Hals (c. 1620), as Clifford Ackley has noted. Clearly, for Rembrandt the figure reaching out from behind a stone, oval frame assumed new symbolic, evocative import in this posthumous context. A preparatory drawing in the British Museum (Benesch 763, figure 4) is more conservative in conception, showing the figure with several books on an adjacent desk behind the frame, the preacher reaching out less aggressively into our space.

The dramatic significance of the print is enhanced by the powerful light cast from above and to the right. In fine impressions like this one, the effect is not merely one of strong shadows but also of extraordinary luminosity, notably in the preacher's hand, which seems translucent, a radiant source in its own right. Through a magnificent range of strokes, webbings and interpenetrations of lines and patterns, through fine touches of drypoint (note the fingers, hair, and velvety fur collar), and especially through the rich and sensitive modulation of tone throughout the plate (note the sleeves and lower vest), Rembrandt directly conveys textures felt and vivid forms perceived in motion through palpable atmosphere. Relying once again on effects achieved by biting into the plate with a sulfur tint (see comments, cat. no. 18), Rembrandt delicately varies the surface tone as though using gray wash. The result is a tenebrous effect heightened by contrast with the whiteness of passages of fine burnishing, as in the preacher's outstretched palm and his eyes.

Around the oval portrait:

Spes mea Christus. Iohannes Cornelij Sylbrius, Amstelodamobat: functus S.S. Minisit: aõs 45. et 6. menses. In Frislâ, in Tyenarum et Phradum aõs 4. In Balc et Harich unicum. In Amorestine aõs 4.

.19. Novembr. natus aõs 74.

ibidemq obijt aõ. 1638.

Amstelodami aõs 28. et 6. menses.

Hollandia, Slotie aõs 6.

Cuius adorandum docuit Facundia Christum,
  Et populis veram pandit ad astra viam.
Talis erat Sylvî facies. audivimus illum
  Amstelijs isto civibus ore loqui.
Hoc Frisijs praecepta dedit; pietasq. severo
  Relligioq. diu vindice tuta stetit.
Praeluxit, veneranda suis virtutibus, aetas.
  Erudytq. ipsos fessa senecta viros.

Simplicitatis amans fucum contemsit honesti,
  Nec sola voluit fronte placere bonis.
Sic statuit: Iesum vita meliore doceri
  Rectiús, et vocum fulmina posse minus.
Amstela, his memor extincti. qui condidit urbem
  Moribus, hanc ipso fulsijt illo Deo.
          C. Barlaeus.
Haud ampliús depraedico illiús dotes,
  Quas aemulor, frustraqué persequor versu.
          P. S.

Figure 5. Rembrandt, *Ephraim Bonus*, Amsterdam, Rijksmuseum

21 Ephraim Bonus, Jewish Physician

Date of execution: 1647

Definitive catalogues: H. 226; B., Holl. 278, state II/II

Process: etching, drypoint, and burin

Data on plate: lower right corner: Rembrandt f. 1647

Data on print: on verso, upper left: B278 (pencil); lower center: c.12001 (pencil); lower right center: B278 (pencil); LB172 (pencil)

Dimensions: 212 mm x 177 mm (8⅜″ x 7″) trimmed within platemark to base of image from bottom of sheet, trimmed to platemark at top
212 mm x 178 mm (8⅜″ x 7¹⁄₁₆″) sheet

Watermarks: –

Collections: Henry Graves & Co. Collection, London (acc. to invoice); (Kennedy Galleries, March 1, 1969)

Ephraim Bonus was an influential and esteemed Portuguese Jewish physician. He was also an underwriter of Manasseh ben Israel's Hebrew publishing firm, so it is not surprising that he became acquainted with Rembrandt. The print was preceded by an unusual procedure for the artist: a painted half-length study of the subject on panel (facing the opposite direction; Amsterdam, Rijksmuseum, figure 5). The existence of the oil sketch would seem to indicate that Rembrandt anticipated extended work on the etching itself.

The composition of the print expands the painted composition on all sides, extends the figure to three-quarter length, and inserts the staircase banister, which effectively sets Bonus within an intimate, specific space (his home?) and contributes to the balance and naturalness of the composition and the stability of the physician's pose. Rembrandt rejects the sense of hurried activity and momentary glance of the oil sketch in favor of a reserved and introspective presentation of the subject. The man of affairs is superseded by the melancholic philosopher.

The quietude and intimacy of Rembrandt's print is also communicated technically, especially in the second state, here exhibited. As is well known, the artist burnished the ring on Bonus's hand so that it appears white. More importantly, he reduced the highlights by shading the banister, the walls, and the physician's clothing to envelop the figure in a cool, even lighting and to reinforce his right contour. Subtle shadows on the wall and banister spatially define the tenebrous space and contribute to the reflective mood of the work. Burin and drypoint delicately delineate the face and the darker shadows of Bonus's clothing. The diverse techniques create a broad range of blacks and grays, of lines, strokes, and flecks of surfaces and volumes perceived, and poignantly evoke Bonus's contemplative mood.

22 Jan Asselyn, Painter ('Krabbetje')

Date of execution: c. 1647

Definitive catalogues: H. 227; B., Holl. 277, state II/III

Process: etching, drypoint, and burin

Data on plate: lower right corner: Rembr f 16(??)

Data on print: on verso, lower left corner: Kn 1205 (diagonally, pencil); below preceding: B.277II (pencil); below preceding: a43484_ (pencil); below preceding: 2112 (pencil)

Dimensions: 187 mm x 169 mm (7⅟₁₆″ x 6¹¹⁄₁₆″) trimmed to platemark on top and sides, the bottom blank margin trimmed off

Watermarks: – (laminated Japanese paper, backed)

Collections: Ralph King, Cleveland, 1855–1926; (Christie's, New York, May 10, 1982, lot 88); (R. E. Lewis, January 25, 1983)

After initial training with the battle-scene painter Isaias van de Velde, Jan Asselyn (1615–1652) traveled to Rome, where he joined the Dutch art community and excelled in landscapes inspired by the early style of Claude Lorrain, a style he brought back to Holland in the 1640s. During his extended stay in Rome he joined a loose, fraternal, and from all accounts highly congenial organization of Dutch artists, the so-called Bentvueghels. Each new member was baptized with wine and given a nickname. Asselyn's, "Krabbetje" (meaning little crab), no doubt referred to his deformed hand. Nonetheless, he seems to have taken to it and used it after his return to Holland in 1645. Asselyn's sister was the wife of Ferdinand Bol, Rembrandt's former pupil.

Rembrandt presents the subject boldly and uncompromisingly, short, stout, with a broad nose. Subtly, however, the artist has manipulated the image. Asselyn's deformed left hand is virtually hidden in dark drapery; his active right hand is highlighted. A tall, Italianate cap augments his height somewhat, an effect heightened in the exhibited second and third states by the burnishing out of an easel (echoing the contours of his hat) and a large, horizontal landscape painting on it that appear in the first state. Their removal adds vertical stature and monumentality to the subject.

In the second state, here printed on a golden-toned, laminated Japanese paper, traces of the earlier composition are still visible on the plate. In the 1640s Rembrandt began to experiment actively in the use of Japanese and Indian papers, interested both in their textures and tonalities and in the softer and more atmospheric effects made possible by their distinctive manners of absorbing ink. This is a particularly fine and luminous impression. Note the rich drypoint on Asselyn's shirt ruff.

22A Jan Asselyn, Painter ('Krabbetje')

Date of execution: c. 1647

Definitive catalogues: H. 227; B., Holl. 277, state III/III

Process: etching, drypoint, and burin

Data on plate: lower right corner: Rembr f 16(??)

Data on print: on verso, lower right center: 124 (pencil); lower right corner: K58 (brown ink)

Dimensions: 217 mm x 170 mm (8⁹⁄₁₆″ x 6¹¹⁄₁₆″) platemark
219 mm x 171 mm (8⅝″ x 6¾″) sheet

Watermarks: –

Collections: (Christie's, New York, November 2, 1983, lot 128)

In the third state all traces of the composition of the first state, some of them still evident in the second state, have been removed through burnishing of the plate. The presence of both the second and third states of this print in the collection provides an interesting opportunity to compare a very good impression of the third state, printed on Western paper, with a brilliant but trimmed impression of the second state printed on laminated Japanese paper (cat. no. 22).

23 Clement de Jonghe, Printseller

Date of execution: 1651
Definitive catalogues: H. 251; B., Holl. 272, state I/VI
Process: etching
Data on plate: lower right corner: Rembrandt f. 1651
Data on print: on verso, upper left corner: 212 (brown ink);
   lower right center: B272I (pencil); lower right: c.3178 (pencil);
   bottom right: c 2257 iiK (pencil); bottom right corner:
   f [over] 14 (brown ink)
Dimensions: 207 mm x 161 mm (8⅛″ x 6⅜″) platemark
            217 mm x 170 mm (8½″ x 6¹¹⁄₁₆″) sheet
Watermarks: (at center?)
Collections: (Sotheby's, London, February 4, 1982, lot 176)

A prominent Amsterdam printseller with a shop on the Kalverstraat, Clement de Jonghe does not appear to have had an extensive business relationship with the artist (only two prints after Rembrandt were published by him). He highly admired the artist's work, however, acquiring a significant personal collection of his etchings. An inventory of that collection at the time of de Jonghe's death provided the first significant catalogue of Rembrandt's printed corpus and became the source for several traditional titles of his works.

As Christopher White has noted, the sober, monumental frontal pose of the merchant clearly reveals the influence of Venetian Renaissance painting on Rembrandt's mature style. By the late 1630s Amsterdam had become an international center for the art trade, and major works by such Italian masters as Raphael, Titian, Tintoretto, and Correggio passed through the city. In one particularly famous drawing now in the Albertina, Vienna (Benesch 451), Rembrandt sketched Raphael's portrait of *Baldassare Castiglione* (Paris, Louvre), which appeared in auction on April 9, 1639. He subsequently synthesized that portrait with Titian's *Man with a Blue Sleeve* (London, National Gallery), a work he knew in the inventory of the art merchant Alfonso Lopez, in an etched self-portrait (1639; B., Holl. 21) and a painted one (1640; London, National Gallery).

By the 1650s, however, Rembrandt had abandoned the bravura and elaborate technical devices of his earlier portraits in favor of a simpler, more monumental style, not dissimilar in spirit to the late portraits of Titian. The subject is presented frontally, enveloped in a cloak defined in a few broad, heavy folds. A high-backed chair lends further stability and classical balance to the composition. The artist also eschews complex patterning for relatively open and loose line work. The depiction is simple, direct, and nondiscursive. By varying his open parallel hatching in direction and proximity, he conveys the intensity and directionality of light and the varied surfaces it touches.

Each of the five states of this print presents noteworthy changes in its characterization of the sitter. In the first state (here exhibited), executed entirely in etching, Rembrandt captures de Jonghe's intellectual acuity, which is powerfully communicated in his intense stare, and his monumental presence in a dramatically focused composition of cool clarity. The sensitive use of plate tone in this impression, with clear wiping scratches, contributes significantly to the atmospheric "tone" and mood of the work. In subsequent states Rembrandt subtly changed the psychological characterization of the subject by adding drypoint and burin to deepen the shadows, especially on the right side of the sitter's face, his hat, and his eyes and along the left edge of the print.

24 Jan Lutma, Goldsmith

Date of execution: 1656
Definitive catalogues: H. 290; B., Holl. 276, state I/III
Process: etching and drypoint
Data on plate: –
Data on print: on verso, lower left: N.L.R. (pencil); 275_(?) (pencil, partially erased); lower right center: LOM (pencil); lower left corner: BF/(pencil); B.276 (pencil); below preceding: LW (pencil); lower right corner: 55 (pencil); below preceding: LAAA (pencil)
Dimensions: 198 mm x 149 mm (7^{13}⁄₁₆″ x 5⅞″) platemark
203 mm x 154 mm (7^{15}⁄₁₆″ x 6¹⁄₁₆″) sheet
Watermarks: large watermark not clearly decipherable (crest?)
Collections: on verso, lower left corner: Lugt 2283 [R. von Seydlitz, Pilgramshain, d. 1870]; lower right corner: Lugt 538d (this print is specifically cited) [G. Cognacq, Paris, 1880–1951]; (R. E. Lewis, January 25, 1983)

The etched portraits of the later 1650s are arguably Rembrandt's greatest. In them he achieves a profound psychological penetration that at once captures his subjects' individuality and transcends them as individuals to become a statement of the human condition. Among the most famous of these late portraits is that of Jan Lutma, presented here in both the first and second states. Lutma, born in Groningen in 1584, moved to Amsterdam in 1621 and established himself as one of the leading goldsmiths and jewelers of his time. His silverwork, shown on the table to his left, was especially prized. Lutma was also an art collector who had visited Rome and owned a large print collection. His son, Jan Lutma the Younger, was an etcher. Lutma is portrayed in his study, surrounded by his tools and creations, holding a small sculpture (his own work?) in his softly highlighted right hand.

The differences between the first and second states of this print are particularly noteworthy, for they reflect a dichotomy in Rembrandt's portraiture between setting his figures in a blank, neutral space (e.g. cat. nos. 5, 13, 18, 22, 23) and setting them in a personalized interior (e.g. cat. nos. 9, 12, 19, 21). In the first state the sitter is set against a large blank wall. In a counterproof of this state, preserved at the Rijksmuseum, Amsterdam, the artist has added gray wash to the background, anticipating the second state (cat. no. 24A).

Rembrandt carefully and distinctively inked different impressions of the print. In this early impression of the first state, a thin film of plate tone imparts a gray tonality to the sheet. The folds in the sleeves of Lutma's cloak are charged with burr, giving them a velvety richness and enhancing the tenebrous atmosphere of the print. Through the central posing of the figure against the high-backed chair and the luminous highlighting of Lutma's head before the blank wall, Rembrandt seeks to focus the composition on the face, so subtly defined in an ambiguous, complex, and poignant expression of mood and thought. Yet by the sensitive application of plate tone he keeps these areas from becoming too brilliantly white and creating a dramatic contrast that would conflict with the overall mood of the portrait.

Figure 6. Jan Lutma the Younger, *Ioannes Lutma Aurifecx*, etching, Hanover, New Hampshire, Hood Museum of Art, Dartmouth College

24A Jan Lutma, Goldsmith

Date of execution: 1656

Definitive catalogues: H. 290; B., Holl. 276, state II/III

Process: etching, drypoint, and burin

Data on plate: top right center in window: Rembrandt f.1656; right center: Joannes Lutma Aurifex / Natus Groningae [this inscription added to the plate by Jan Lutma the Younger]

Data on print: on verso, top center: 94 (pencil); lower center: II (pencil); below preceding: B276 (pencil); lower right: 256 (pencil); below preceding: 25_(?) (pencil); lower left corner: A 321 CWHC (pencil); bottom center: 21 919 3568 (pencil)

Dimensions: 199 mm x 149 mm (7⅞″ x 5⅞″) platemark
202 mm x 152 mm (8″ x 6″) sheet

Watermarks: –

Collections: (Kennedy Galleries, December 30, 1969)

As noted in the previous entry, Rembrandt made a preparatory study leading to interesting and significant changes between the first and second states of this portrait. This is a particularly fine impression of the second state, with much burr and plate tone yet great clarity. By adding the alcove with a window behind the sitter, Rembrandt has not only placed him within a more personal and intimate setting, but also enhanced the consistency of tone and the harmony between the interior space and the solemnity of the portrait. More subtle changes include the sensitive additional work on Lutma's face; the softening of the shadows on the adjacent table, which brings his professional attributes into greater clarity; the lightly etched beaker on the sill, which softens the sharp rectilinearity of the window frame; and the inclusion of Rembrandt's signature and date. Rembrandt has also softened the shadow of the chair on the near wall to the far left. The overall effect is one of more even and tenebrous lighting.

The sensitivity and subtlety of Rembrandt's portrayal of Lutma is all the more apparent when the work is compared with an etching of the same subject executed in the same year by Jan Lutma the Younger, a print clearly based on Rembrandt's composition (figure 6).

Mythology, Allegory, and the Human Figure

25 The Small Lion Hunt (with One Lion)

Date of execution: c. 1629

Definitive catalogues: H. 6; B., Holl. 116, state I/I

Process: etching

Data on plate: –

Data on print: on verso, upper left corner: ___Gt. (pencil); below preceding: ___Derde (pencil); lower right corner: Ex. vs (pencil); center at base: 50484 (pencil)

Dimensions: 156 mm x 116 mm (6⅛″ x 4⅝″) platemark
        160 mm x 122 mm (6⁵⁄₁₆″ x 4¹³⁄₁₆″) sheet

Watermarks: –

Collections: on verso, lower left corner: Lugt 1879 [Mrs. M. J. Morgan, New York, d. before 1886]; Boies Penrose, 1937 (acc. to invoice); Gordon Nowell-Usticke (Sotheby Parke Bernet, New York, lot 386, sale 1968, acc. to inv.); (Lucien Gold-schmidt, January 29, 1986)

The Small Lion Hunt is among the earliest of Rembrandt's genre scenes and the most dramatic of his early prints. Employing sharp light and dark contrasts, energized by the violent, frenzied strokes of the etching needle, Rembrandt found the inspiration for this print not so much in the works of Rubens, that earlier Northern Baroque master who explored the theme, but in those of the Italian proto-Baroque painter and printmaker Antonio Tempesta (1555–1630; Bartsch 1135, figure 7; also Bartsch 1123), an artist who specialized in battle and hunting scenes. Four volumes of prints by Tempesta are listed in the inventory taken of Rembrandt's extensive art collection in connection with his 1656 bankruptcy.

Abandoning Tempesta's carefully defined contours and complex compositional design in favor of a sharp diagonal pyramid of figures and a brilliant contrast of intense light against a shadow in which the figures merge, Rembrandt captures far more of the fury of the hunt than the older artist had. By simplifying the composition of Tempesta and amplifying the figures in broad, rough, even crude strokes, Rembrandt augments the senses of immediacy, spontaneity of action, and violence. The present etching, printed on a warm, golden-tan paper, is a fine, early, and richly inked impression with plate tone and many wiping scratches.

Figure 7. Antonio Tempesta, *Lion Hunt*, etching, Paris, Bibliothèque Nationale

Figure 8. Jacques Callot, *Beggar*, etching, London, British Museum

Figure 9. Rembrandt, *Self Portrait Open Mouthed, As If Shouting: Bust*, etching, state I/III, Paris, Bibliothèque Nationale

26 Beggar Seated on a Bank

Date of execution: 1630
Definitive catalogues: H. 11; B., Holl. 174, state I/I
Process: etching
Data on plate: bottom center: RHL (monogram) 1630
Data on print: on recto, lower right corner: 168 (brown ink); on verso, top left center: W171 (pencil); lower left corner: 171 (pencil); bottom center: 203 (red chalk)
Dimensions: 117 mm x 71 mm (4⁹⁄₁₆″ x 2¹³⁄₁₆″) platemark
119 mm x 74 mm (4¹¹⁄₁₆″ x 2¹⁵⁄₁₆″) sheet
Watermarks: –
Collections: on verso, lower left center: Lugt 176 [H. Danby Seymour, London and Trent, 1820–1877]; (Sotheby's, London, January 26, 1979, lot 940)

The subject of beggars appears often in the early figure studies of Rembrandt. They had, of course, previously been portrayed in the works of sixteenth-century Netherlandish artists, notably Bosch and Bruegel, but less as studies of suffering human beings than as naturalistically observed figure types, automata acting out prescribed moralistic allegories and narratives. Generally viewed with derision, such figures were seen as picturesque characters. Rembrandt was fascinated, however, with the humanity and diverse experiences expressed in the faces and physiognomy of the elderly, the destitute and wandering beggars who lived on the fringes of society and were readily found in Leyden and Amsterdam.

In his earliest studies, Rembrandt was influenced by the celebrated series of etchings of beggars by Jacques Callot, which was published in the 1620s and well-circulated by 1630 (e.g. Lieure 490, figure 8). Unlike Callot's etched, theatrical presentation of his subjects, however, in Rembrandt's prints we find a rejection of elegant, fluid design, parallel hatching, and clear contours. His figures possess greater naturalism and personality; they constitute a humanity of suffering individuals rather than symbolic embodiments of strife.

It is no wonder, therefore, that among these early images of beggars we should find a self-portrait. At the time of these etchings Rembrandt was portraying himself in a series of uncompromising self-portraits, in which he examines human expression and emotion (B., Holl. 13, figure 9; see comments, cat. no. 4) for use in his narrative paintings. Unshaven and unkempt, Rembrandt places himself seated outdoors on a ledge, wearing old, half-rotted shoes. The natural light obscures part of his face and the contours of his old, ragged coat. His facial grimace is similar to that in the self-portrait, yet in this context it assumes a fierce, poignant intensity as the half-crazed, elemental cry of a suffering young beggar.

Figure 10. Jacques Callot, *The Two Pilgrims*, etching, London, British Museum

27 Beggar Man and Woman Behind a Bank

Date of execution: c. 1630

Definitive catalogues: H. 13; B., Holl. 165, state VIII/IX

Process: etching, drypoint, and burin

Data on plate: –

Data on print: on verso, upper left corner: 17585 (pencil); upper center: 6th (pencil); center: B.165 VIII (pencil); H 13 VI (pencil); lower center: C.22801 (pencil); lower left: j/B.165 (pencil); bottom left corner: c. 101___(?) (pencil); bottom center: 150 (pencil); lower right corner: Mu___(?) 15D (pencil)

Dimensions: 98 mm x 68 mm (3⅞″ x 2¹¹⁄₁₆″) platemark
             100 mm x 70 mm (3¹⁵⁄₁₆″ x 2¾″) sheet

Watermarks: –

Collections: on verso, lower right: Lugt 1119b [A. J. Godby, Baltimore and London, 1853–1934]; (Lucien Goldschmidt, January 27, 1986)

In the *Beggar Man and Woman Behind a Bank* Rembrandt effectively applies his increased mastery of the technique of etching to express eloquently the suffering of the two elderly beggars. How different the sensibility is from that of his contemporary, Jacques Callot (Lieure 481, figure 10; see comments, cat. no. 26)! The bank in the foreground forms a dramatic repoussoir, a curtain from behind which the couple falteringly emerge. Rembrandt attempts to create a transition between the wedge-like rocky outcropping and the sensitively defined figures through the deep shading of the old man's left shoulder.

The print is an early example of the effects Rembrandt achieved by exposing some sections of the plate to the acid bath longer than others, creating the evident range in tones. He also has used drypoint and burin to enrich the shadows, especially in the bank. The artist created no fewer than nine states of this print, of which this is the eighth, constantly readjusting the shading, darkening the highlights, and adding touches of drypoint to the figures. On two occasions (the second and fifth states) he cut down the height of the plate, from 116 mm to 113 mm to 98 mm. The faces are among the most eloquent expressions of misery ever created by the artist.

28 Man in a Cloak and Fur Cap Leaning Against a Bank

Date of execution: c. 1630

Definitive catalogues: H. 14; B., Holl. 151, state I/III

Process: etching

Data on plate: upper right corner: RHL (monogram, reversed)

Data on print: on verso, lower right corner: VBAS (pencil); bottom center: B 151 (pencil)

Dimensions: 113 mm x 79 mm (4⁷⁄₁₆″ x 3⅛″) platemark
135 mm x 95 mm (5⁵⁄₁₆″ x 3¾″) sheet

Watermarks: partial fleur-de-lys in a shield

Collections: on verso, lower left corner: Lugt 271 and Lugt 1442 [both, J. D. Böhm, Vienna, 1794–1865]; Gordon Nowell-Usticke (Sotheby Parke Bernet, New York, May 6, 1969, lot 44); (Sotheby Parke Bernet, New York, February 15, 1980, lot 1091)

As in his contemporary so-called portraits of his father (cat. nos. 2, 3), Rembrandt is here attracted to genre images of the elderly for the richness of experience that their faces and bodies could bring to his repertoire of figure types to be appropriated as dramatis personae of his religious and historical works (see cat. nos. 44, 46, 47). The artist can be seen to be progressing rapidly in his mastery and control of the medium and of composition, achieving a more coherent sense of space, volume, and mass in this etching than in either cat. no. 26 or 27.

29 Old Beggar Woman with a Gourd

Date of execution: c. 1630
Definitive catalogues: H. 80; B., Holl. 168, state II/II
Process: etching
Data on plate: –
Data on print: on verso, lower left: f3553/a (pencil); bottom center: B.168 (58) (pencil)
Dimensions: 104 mm x 48 mm (4⅛″ x 1¹⁵⁄₁₆″) trimmed to platemark
Watermarks: –
Collections: on verso, lower left corner: Lugt 1250 [J. C. D. Hebich, Hamburg, 1818–1891]; upper center: Lugt 1681ter [F. A. Lieberg, Buenos Aires, b. 1898]; lower center: unidentified collection mark, featuring the blind letters of a capital Gothic *T*, a lowercase *h*, and a capital Gothic *F* (or *H*) against a rectangular, framed, black ground; (Sotheby's, London, February 4, 1982, lot 168)

The *Old Beggar Woman with a Gourd* was placed by Hind in the Rembrandt corpus after cat. no. 31; however, the rough etching strokes, the use of sharp light-to-dark contrasts, the clear contours, the picturesque depiction of the ragged woman, focusing on the gourd and setting the face in darkly shadowed profile—characteristics close to Callot in sensibility—indicate a date of execution roughly contemporary with cat. no. 28 and marginally earlier than cat. no. 30, c. 1629–30. In the second state, presented here, the artist cut down the plate slightly and added the horizontal line near the base, setting the figure more convincingly in space.

30 Ragged Peasant with His Hands Behind Him, Holding a Stick

Date of execution: c. 1630

Definitive catalogues: H. 16; B., Holl. 172, state V/VI

Process: etching and drypoint

Data on plate: –

Data on print: on verso, upper left corner: 105 GL. (pencil);
lower center: #87741 (pencil); lower left: 4991. (pencil); below
preceding: vs/h (pencil); lower left corner: O20UA (pencil);
bottom center: B172 (pencil)

Dimensions: 91 mm x 67 mm (3⅝″ x 2¹¹⁄₁₆″) platemark
97 mm x 73 mm (3¹³⁄₁₆″ x 2⅞″) sheet

Watermarks: partial indecipherable mark (top of a crown?)

Collections: on verso, lower left center: Lugt 68 [A. F. T.
Bohnenberger, Stuttgart, 1826–1893]; bottom center: Lugt
345 [Cabinet Bretano-Birkenstock, Vienna and Frankfort];
center: Lugt 1760b [L. J. Rosenwald, Philadelphia, b. 1891];
Lugt 1932d [Washington, National Gallery of Art]; National
Gallery of Art duplicate (Sotheby's, London, June 14, 1984,
lot 156)

This is another beggar study characterized by the same
rapid, parallel hatching of the etching needle used in the
three preceding catalogued prints. Rembrandt's approach
to his subject matter, however, has become increasingly
sympathetic and personalized. Far from the picturesque
caricatures of Callot, Rembrandt represents beggars with
warmth and empathy as human beings, integrating them
into the Dutch social framework by making their experience
psychologically accessible to the viewer. He also rejects the
crisp contours, continuous profiles, and sharp light-to-dark
contrast of the French artist, relying increasingly on the
middle range of shadows, as though the forms are seen
in the natural outdoor light of the Netherlands. These
more sophisticated modulations of light reflect a greater
mastery of technique. It was Rembrandt's understanding
vision of the lower social classes that inspired such artists as
Adriaen van Ostade, Jan Miel, and Abraham Bloemart.

31 Jupiter and Antiope: Smaller Plate

Date of execution: c. 1631

Definitive catalogues: H. 44; B., Holl. 204, state II/II

Process: etching and burin

Data on plate: right center: RHL (monogram)

Data on print: on verso, lower left: (14)(pencil); [4]SW (pencil);
below preceding: ⚠ DED (pencil); below preceding: 14111
(pencil); lower left corner: ☐ ny (pencil); bottom
center: <u>433</u> (pencil)

Dimensions: 85 mm x 113 mm (3⁵⁄₁₆″ x 4⁷⁄₁₆″) platemark
87 mm x 115 mm (3⁷⁄₁₆″ x 4½″) sheet

Watermarks: –

Collections: on verso, lower left corner: Lugt 33 [August
Artaria, Vienna, 1807–1893]; (Sotheby's, London, November
19, 1982, lot 585)

As Christopher White has noted, this print has been
conceived as a series of poignant contrasts: male and
female, age and youth, activity and passivity, lechery and
innocence, dark and light. The subject is almost certainly
that of Jupiter (who with rare appropriateness has assumed
the form of a satyr; see Ovid, *Metamorphoses*, VI, 111)
entering from outdoors to ravish the sleeping Antiope,
pushing aside the bed curtains. Although the print also
has been called "Venus and a Satyr" (notably in Clement
de Jonghe's 1679 inventory and Gersaint's 1751 catalogue
raisonné), the aged and crowned male figure looming out
of the shadows and the sleeping, naturalistic, and un-
idealized female nude correspond faithfully—if not very
becomingly for the king of the gods—to the myth of
Jupiter and Antiope. The subject, of course, had been
a favorite of such Renaissance masters as Titian and
Correggio, but Rembrandt's wry, sardonic presentation of
the theme is totally different in sensibility from the elevated
eroticism of the Italian artists' works, despite the warm
and intense highlighting of the nude Antiope. (On Werner
van der Valckert's etching *Sleeping Venus Surprised by
Satyrs*, 1612, which is considered a compositional source
for this print, see C. Ackley, *Printmaking in the Age of
Rembrandt*, Boston: Museum of Fine Arts, 1981, cat. no.
47 [repr.], pp. 79–81.)

In this early etching Rembrandt still has some difficulty
in projecting Antiope's legs in foreshortening. In the
second state, exhibited here, he camouflages this problem
with the addition of the blanket. The modeling of her
outstretched arm also lacks conviction.

32 The Quacksalver

Date of execution: 1635
Definitive catalogues: H. 139; B., Holl. 129, state I/I
Process: etching
Data on plate: lower center: Rembrandt.f.1635
Data on print: –
Dimensions: 78 mm x 36 mm (3¹⁄₁₆″ x 1⁷⁄₁₆″) platemark
          80 mm x 40 mm (3³⁄₁₆″ x 1⁹⁄₁₆″) sheet
Watermarks: –
Collections: (Karl und Faber, Munich, auction 145, May 26–28,
    1977, lot 280)

Certainly among the most delightful and fanciful of
Rembrandt's subjects, *The Quacksalver* of 1635 is also
notable for the artist's ability to capture a seemingly
spontaneous moment of activity, when the peddler is in
the midst of delivering his "pitch," unselfconscious and
unposed. In two famous drawings of c. 1637, one in the
collection of the Berlin-Dahlem Kupferstichkabinet
(Benesch 416) and the other at the Courtauld Gallery,
London (ex-collection Count Antoine Seilern, Benesch
417), the figure of a quacksalver is shown on a stage
haranguing the public and enunciating the dubious
benefits of his wares, a large poster or chart hanging on
the scrim behind him. In the present study the figure,
dressed with imaginative panache but somewhat archaic
attire, is depicted singly but in the midst of a harangue to
an unseen clientele. Rembrandt not only conveys the
humorous, anecdotal character of the moment, but achieves
a social and psychological penetration akin to what we
find in his sketches of beggars.

Figure 11. Rembrandt, *Three Studies of a Beggar*, pen and brown ink, London, British Museum

Figure 12. Jacques Callot, *Beggar on Crutches*, etching, London, British Museum

33 A Peasant in a High Cap, Standing Leaning on a Stick

Date of execution: 1639

Definitive catalogues: H. 164; B., Holl. 133, state I/I

Process: etching

Data on plate: lower center: Rembrandt f.1639

Data on print: on verso, lower left center: 133 (pencil)

Dimensions: 83 mm x 44 mm (3¼″ x 1¾″) platemark
           86 mm x 47 mm (3⅜″ x 1⅞″) sheet

Watermarks: –

Collections: (Christie's, New York, November 2, 1983, lot 120);
   (W. H. Schab, November 25, 1983)

The figure in this print is sometimes identified as a Jew, but that characterization is incorrect, since drawn studies of similar figures of elderly beggars in high hats on the march or begging alms can be found in the artist's corpus extending back to his Leyden years (Benesch 14, 43) as well as his early Amsterdam period (as in the *Three Studies of a Beggar*, c. 1636, London, British Museum, Benesch 327, figure 11). Callot also depicted beggars similarly attired (Lieure 488, figure 12). The continued conflicts of the Thirty Years War undoubtedly contributed to the timeliness of the subject.

This print is very rare; only eight impressions are known. The present impression is a clear, early impression before scratches appear on the plate. It was printed slightly drily on the left side.

34 The Artist Drawing from the Model

Date of execution: c. 1639

Definitive catalogues: H. 231; B., Holl. 192, state II/II

Process: etching, drypoint, and burin

Data on plate: –

Data on print: on verso, lower left: L. 906 (pencil); below
   preceding: 10998 (pencil); lower center: B. 192 (pencil); lower
   left corner: B.C. Nr. 192 (pencil); lower right: 71220 (pencil);
   below preceding: N E (pencil); bottom center: cat 58 (pencil);
   lower right corner: 6. (pencil)

Dimensions: 231 mm x 184 mm (9¹⁄₁₆″ x 7³⁄₁₆″) platemark
   237 mm x 189 mm (9⁵⁄₁₆″ x 7½″) sheet

Watermarks: partial fleur-de-lys

Collections: on verso, lower left: Lugt 906 [Ed. Schultze, Vienna,
   d. c. 1900]; (Sotheby's, London, May 15, 1986, lot 76)

Figure 13. Rembrandt, *The Artist Drawing from a Model*, pen
and brown ink and wash, London, British Museum

Owing to its incompletion, *The Artist Drawing from the
Model* remains among the most haunting and evocative
of Rembrandt's subjects. A genre depiction of an artist
drawing from his model in his studio, with various professional props and tools mounted against the back wall,
is thereby transformed into a reflection on the creative
process itself. It is not surprising, therefore, that in the
Netherlands the print also traditionally bore the title of
The Statue of Pygmalion (first so recorded by the Dutch
merchant Pierre Yver in 1756 as a notation in his supplement to Gersaint's 1751 catalogue raisonné); and
Rembrandt apparently was influenced in his composition
by an etching of that mythological subject by Pieter Feddes.
Rembrandt's preparatory drawing for the print, preserved
at the British Museum (Benesch 423, figure 13) is in the
same direction as Feddes's print and similarly depicts a
nude female model on a pedestal holding drapery. As in
his *Jupiter and Antiope* (cat. no. 31), however, which was
similarly influenced by a print by van der Valckert of
Sleeping Venus Surprised by Satyrs, Rembrandt has felt
free to recast both composition and subject. The story
of Pygmalion hardly seems to be the subject of the print,
not only because of the narrative ambiguity of the composition, but also because the depicted artist is a draftsman
rather than a sculptor.

The unfinished plate also reveals Rembrandt's working
method. In the preparatory drawing he rapidly sketches
in the contours of the figures, with only the briefest
suggestions of shading. The studio background, however, so
carefully worked up in the unfinished plate, is already
sensitively laid in with washes to convey in warm shadows
its depth. In the etching plate Rembrandt sketches in the
figures with drypoint. Their poses and heights are still
not resolved in the second state (note the two pairs of feet
on the model). The artist is brought forward and given
greater prominence than in his pose in the preparatory
drawing. In the second state Rembrandt also introduces
further shading in the upper portion of the print, notably

darkening the upper section of the easel at the center of
the composition and the looming female bust and chimney
on the right. The scene thus becomes totally enclosed and
nocturnal. Minor additions to the lower half of the
composition include the further definition of the drapery
over the model's arm and the addition of shading below
the lower edge of the canvas on the easel. The unfinished
foreground remains luminous, its mystery and suggestive-
ness enhanced by the profound darkness of the surrounding
studio.

35 The Large Lion Hunt

Date of execution: 1641
Definitive catalogues: H. 181; B., Holl. 114, state II/II
Process: etching and drypoint
Data on plate: upper right: Rembrandt f 1641
Data on print: on verso, bottom center: B.114II (pencil); below
    preceding: c.28899 (pencil)
Dimensions: 224 mm x 298 mm (8¹³⁄₁₆″ x 11¹¹⁄₁₆″) platemark
    234 mm x 309 mm (9³⁄₁₆″ x 12³⁄₁₆″) sheet
Watermarks: crown with letters IFD (very similar to Churchill 5)
Collections: (Sotheby Parke Bernet, New York, November 14,
    1981, lot 846)

In *The Large Lion Hunt* the mature artist returns to
one of the earliest themes of his career (see cat. no. 25).
Again he has studied the prints of Antonio Tempesta
(especially Bartsch 1149). While still using an open and
free drawing style, thereby enhancing the dynamic energy
and sense of spontaneous drama in the print, Rembrandt
demonstrates far greater control over his medium than
in the work of 1629. A coherent and consistent light falls
on the figures, and the spatial recession is far more convincingly presented. The composition is more complex
than in the early work, but is also more clearly defined. The
entire rotary organization and focus of the composition
about the central slaying of the lions is far more sophisticated in conception. Rembrandt's understanding and
summary articulation of equine and lion anatomy is
extraordinary. Although Persian miniatures depicting
hunting scenes, works that Rembrandt collected, have been
cited as his inspiration, it is obvious that the artist made
many studies from life, a fact confirmed by his contemporary drawings of lions (Benesch 774–76). The central
rearing horse derives from a drawing of c. 1635 (Benesch 98).

The impression exhibited is a fine, early impression of
the second state of the print, in which Rembrandt added
some shadow with burin about the head of the horse on
the extreme right to deepen the space. A fine film of plate
tone, notable burr on the fallen rider and elsewhere
throughout the print, and fine wiping scratches also
confirm that this impression was pulled early in the
second state.

36 The Flute Player (L'Espiègle)

Date of execution: 1642

Definitive catalogues: H. 200; B., Hol. 188, state IV/IV

Process: etching and drypoint

Data on plate: bottom center: Rembrandt. f 1642 (the 2 reversed)

Data on print: on verso, lower center: 26/_ (pencil); lower
   right, diagonally up to right: vfg84/pafga (in pencil); lower
   left corner: 517 (pencil); bottom right center: D. Bollefeigh(?)
   C_ K ☐ oo (pencil)

Dimensions: 116 mm x 143 mm (4⁹⁄₁₆″ x 5⅝″) platemark
   117 mm x 146 mm (4⅝″ x 5¾″) sheet

Watermarks: –

Collections: on verso, upper right center: Lugt 2000 [Budapest
   National Gallery, print room]; (Christie's, London, June 17,
   1981, lot 100)

The Flute Player, known since the eighteenth century as
"L'Espiègle" (originally a French contraction of the name
of the popular comic character Til Eulenspiegel), undoubtedly derived this alternative title from the presence
of an owl on the shoulder of the shepherd (Eulenspiegel
translates as "mirror of an owl"). Pastoral poems, notably
those of Vondel, were much in vogue in Holland during
the 1640s; however, more probably the image should be
understood as an erotic allegory. A young shepherdess
wearing a beautifully rendered straw hat (note how the
radiating strokes convey both the subtle variation of
shadows and the texture and structure of straw) sits
stringing a daisy chain. A shepherd seated to her left holds
a flute, the erotic symbolism of which is obvious, while he
is absorbed in looking up her skirt. On his shoulder is
perched an owl, traditionally associated in Dutch art
with magic, filth, and nocturnal activity, while, behind
the shepherd, horned goats, symbolic of lust, frolic by the
water. The scene is set in a summer landscape of great
beauty.

Rembrandt may have been influenced in his composition
by Venetian sources, notably prints after designs by Titian.
A shepherd of the same visage, playing a flute, appears in
a series of prints after a drawing by Titian, notably an
etching of the late sixteenth century by Marco Angelo del
Moro. Titian's celebrated and often reproduced *Three
Ages of Man* of c. 1513 (in 1642 in Augsburg and now on
extended loan to the National Gallery of Scotland, Edin-
burgh) and his late *Nymph and the Shepherd* of c. 1570
(then in the collection of the Duke of Hamilton, London,
and now in Vienna at the Kunsthistorisches Museum)
both present erotically a shepherd and a shepherdess in a
bucolic setting and include flutes and goats. They may
have been known to Rembrandt through intermediary
sources. (On Rembrandt's collection of prints after Titian,
see comments, cat. no. 68.)

Rembrandt executed four states of this print, of which
the final state is here exhibited. His reworking of the
plate reflects his interest in tonal effects and in establishing
the three-dimensional presence of the human figures
against the background. Most of his reworking was devoted
to the hat of the shepherdess, accented in drypoint, and
to the shading (partially burnished out in the second state
only to be restrengthened in the third) of the bower
above her head and behind her. In the fourth state
Rembrandt has redrawn the foreground vegetation and
removed the lightly etched head of another male looking
off to his left from above the bank, just to the right of
the shepherd's staff. Even in this most idyllic of subjects,
Rembrandt's sensibilities are never far from elemental
human emotions.

37 The Bathers

Date of execution: 1651

Definitive catalogues: H. 250; B., Holl. 195, state II/II

Process: etching

Data on plate: lower left corner: Rembrandt. f. 1651 (the 5 is corrected in drypoint from a 3)

Data on print: on verso, bottom right: 33394 (pencil)

Dimensions: 109 mm x 137 mm (4⁵⁄₁₆″ x 5⁷⁄₁₆″) platemark
113 mm x 142 mm (4⁷⁄₁₆″ x 5⁹⁄₁₆″) sheet

Watermarks: –

Collections: on verso, upper center: Lugt 2133 [F. Rechberger, Vienna, 1771–1841], dated in pen and ink 1799; lower left: AW (pencil) [Adolph Weil, Jr., Montgomery, Alabama]; (Karl und Faber, Munich, auction 143, May 1976, lot 210)

The Bathers, certainly among the most unusual of Rembrandt's subjects, is first described in de Jonghe's 1679 inventory as "Swemmertjens." Its naturalistic depiction of male nude bathers (influenced by such Renaissance precedents as Marcantonio Raimondi's *The Climbers* [Bartsch 487]) is a reflection of Rembrandt's intense interest in the physical world. In the late 1640s he executed several drawn and etched studies of male nudes (e.g. B., Holl. 194, which features the same thin male model who appears in the water in the foreground of the present print). The etching must have been conceived as a rough personal study, a rapid sketch, hardly finished, with such unposed and disarmingly veristic observations as the shivering man crouched in the foreground and the nude in the distance covering himself. The second state is distinguished from the first by the regularizing of the edges of the plate, an acid stain at the upper center, and some small scratches on the plate.

Rembrandt. f. 1651

38 Peasant Family on the Tramp

Date of execution: c. 1652
Definitive catalogues: H. 259; B., Holl. 131, state II/II
Process: etching
Data on plate: –
Data on print: on verso, bottom center: B.131 (pencil); bottom
    right: 15 (pencil)
Dimensions: 113 mm x 93 mm (4⁷⁄₁₆″ x 3¹¹⁄₁₆″) platemark
    117 mm x 98 mm (4⅝″ x 3⅞″) sheet
Watermarks: partial (shield?)
Collections: on verso, lower left corner: AW (pencil) [Adolph
    Weil, Jr., Montgomery, Alabama]; (Karl und Faber, Munich,
    auction 142, November 28, 1975, lot 239)

In the lightly etched *Peasant Family on the Tramp* of
the early 1650s we can see how very far Rembrandt has
come in his humanistic empathy with beggar and indigent
subjects from the etchings of the late 1620s (see cat. nos.
26–30). All traces of caricature and picturesque detailing
have been eschewed. Neither does the artist seek to evoke
our commiseration or sympathy through a poignant
expression of suffering. Rather, the figures, despite their
humble state (note the barefoot mother), are presented
simply and forthrightly as a family, immediately accessible
to our own experience, with charm, wit, and tenderness.
Expressions and gestures subtly convey their familial
relations.

Unburnished traces of indecipherable work on the plate
are visible by the man's staff. The second state is distinguished from the first by the correction of some false
biting on the backpack of the father.

39 Faust

Date of execution: c. 1652

Definitive catalogues: H. 260; B., Holl. 270, state II/III

Process: etching and drypoint

Data on plate: –

Data on print: on verso, upper left corner: 2 (pencil); lower center: B.270II (pencil); lower left corner: U Elg (pencil); lower right: EU (pencil)

Dimensions: 210 mm x 160 mm (8¼″ x 6⁵⁄₁₆″) platemark
215 mm x 164 mm (8⁷⁄₁₆″ x 6⁷⁄₁₆″) sheet

Watermarks: CDG (Claude de George)

Collections: Dr. Carlos Gaa (Lugt 538A, Germany, 1871–c.1925, no stamp); (C. G. Boerner, Leipzig, May 1926); on verso, lower left: purple collection stamp of Felix Somary (Vienna and Zurich, 1881–1956); (N. G. Stogdon, Somary Sale, cat. no. 38, November 14, 1985)

It is unlikely that the so-called *Faust* actually portrays the legendary figure immortalized by the 1588 play of Marlowe and the much later work of Goethe. Although there is as yet no definitive interpretation of the subject, the earliest known title for the print, "practiserende alchimist," which appears in Clement de Jonghe's 1679 inventory (no. 33), may well come closest to accuracy. The traditional title is first found in Röver's collection inventory (1731 [see comments, cat. no. 10]) and is repeated in Gersaint's 1751 catalogue raisonné. There, "le Portrait d'un Philosophe, ou Médecin, connu en Hollande sous le nom du docteur Fautrieus" (the title of a seventeenth-century Dutch adaptation of Marlowe's play) is applied to the print.

In a study a scholar rises from his work to gaze intently toward the window, where a mystical symbol and its mirrored counterpart, foreshortened in perspective, appear. The latter is indicated by the arm and pointing finger of a spectral presence, whose head is embodied in the mystical disk. The inspiration of the scholar appears to be divine rather than infernal. At the center of the luminous disk the anagram INRI certainly refers to Christ. About the central circle are the words ALGAR/ALGASTNA AMRTET/ DALGRAM ADAM TE. These incomprehensible words appear on an amulet, now lost, that Rembrandt copied (see H. M. Rotermund, "Untersuchungen zu Rembrandts Faustradierung," *Oud Holland*, 1957, pp. 151ff., and H. Van de Waal, "Rembrandt's *Faust* Etching: A Socinian Document and the Iconography of the Inspired Scholar," *Oud Holland*, 1964, pp. 7ff.).

The composition would seem to be a synthesis of two conventional subjects: the scholar in his study (as in the artist's painting *Philosopher in Meditation*, Paris, Louvre, figure 14, whose date has been read variously as 1631, 1632, or 1633) and the evangelist inspired by an angel. It has been suggested that the subject is related to the ideas of religious inspiration of the Mennonite sect, or alternatively to the mystically inspired, quasi-scientific researches of an alchemist (it should be remembered that in the sixteenth and seventeenth centuries alchemy encompassed the disciplines of medicine, chemistry, and cosmography as well as astrology and mysticism). Whatever his specific iconographic intention, the artist has rendered a moment of mystical revelation in unforgettably luminous terms. The rich shadows of the study, the skull on the sill (a *memento mori*) echoing the head of the scholar, the velvety inking of the drypoint in the scholar's sleeves and cloak, Rembrandt's sensitive use of the white of the paper to realize the brilliant mystical light, and the extraordinary, glistening inking of this superb impression are orchestrated consummately in this masterpiece of the artist's maturity.

Formerly owned by Felix Somary, this impression entered that esteemed collection on the recommendation of Meder. In the second state, here presented, Rembrandt has added fine shading throughout the print to enhance the brilliance of the disk.

Figure 14. Rembrandt, *Philosopher in Meditation*, Paris, Louvre

40 The Golf Player

Date of execution: 1654
Definitive catalogues: H. 272; B., Holl. 125, state I/II
Process: etching
Data on plate: lower left: Rembrandt f.1654
Data on print: on verso, upper right corner: 38 (pencil); lower
     center: Sport of Kobf or Golf (pencil); below preceding: 121
     (pencil); lower left corner: Loo m276 (pencil)
Dimensions: 96 mm x 143 mm (3¹³⁄₁₆″ x 5⅝″) platemark
                  98 mm x 144 mm (3⅞″ x 5¹¹⁄₁₆″) sheet
Watermarks: top center: indecipherable partial watermark
Collections: (Lucien Goldschmidt, December 18, 1980)

The Golf Player, an informal genre study of Rembrandt's
maturity, is actually a composite of three different studies:
the foreground figure in meditation sitting inside an inn
and resting on a bench and an adjacent table on which
stands a beer stein; a figure playing golf; and two figures
in conversation seen through the sketched aperture. The
print also juxtaposes open, loose sketch work with detailed
shading. At this time Rembrandt was studying the prints
of the early Renaissance master Mantegna (see cat. no. 61)
and was influenced by his use of parallel hatching. Using
this open work technique, Rembrandt achieves subtle
wash-like modulations of tone in the interior space.
Christopher White has associated the composition and
broken line work with such contemporary reed pen
drawings as the *Young Man Reclining Asleep* (London,
British Museum, Benesch 1092).

In an unusually detailed discussion in his catalogue
raisonné, Gersaint (1751, cat. no. 121, pp. 106–8) provides
a complete description of the game, popular in Holland
but unknown in eighteenth-century France. Since that
text is of some interest but rarely cited, it is here reproduced in my translation from the French:

The game of golf [*Kolef*] is very common in Holland and little
known in France: those who have country homes often have
playing fields in their yards, but normally they are found at
suburban or country inns where the middle classes go to relax.
They are more or less large: between 8 and 12 fathoms [*toises*]
long and 9 to 10 feet wide. The field where one plays is
ordinarily groomed and enclosed, like our malls. Many can
play in teams, one against the other. There is at each end of the
field, in the middle, a piece of wood about two feet in diameter
and raised two feet, six inches [*pouces*]. One plays with balls
of the size of our tennis balls, which you push with a mallet
[*bâton*], the end of which is covered with lead and is shaped
like a cross. To commence, the balls are placed at one end of the
field. The goal is to be able to first strike the wooden post at
the opposite end of the course. It is rare, because of the distance,
to be able to do this on the first strike, but one tries to place
the ball as close and advantageously as possible to touch the
post on the second strike. If in striking it the player is adroit
or vigorous enough for the ball to bounce back near the other
wooden post at the other end of the field, so that he can touch
it on the third strike (rather than requiring a fourth), the
player then is almost certain to win a match, because the winner
is the one who touches the two wooden posts in the least
number of strikes back and forth. From time to time one finds
players sufficiently adroit to touch both of them in only two
strikes. Sometimes the game is played in parties of two against
two or four against four, in which case a large match ensues.

41   The Goldsmith

Date of execution: 1655

Definitive catalogues: H. 285; B., Holl. 123, state I/II

Process: etching and drypoint

Data on plate: lower left corner: Rembrandt f. 1655

Data on print: on verso, vertically on left margin: NY68-b-ba
   Ger 119 (pencil); center: Klein Gondtratt(?) (pencil); below
   preceding: 28123 (pencil); below preceding: no8 (pencil);
   below preceding: c.26929 (pencil); below preceding: no 31
   os (pencil); lower right: B.128I; H.293 (pencil); below
   preceding: (N 321) (pencil); below preceding: 2200 (pencil);
   center base: 143 (pencil); lower right corner: 14¹⁰ (pencil)

Dimensions: 77 mm x 57 mm (3″ x 2¼″) platemark
                    87 mm x 67 mm (3⁷⁄₁₆″ x 2⅝″) sheet

Watermarks: –

Collections: (Kennedy Galleries, December 30, 1969)

This print of 1655 is the last of Rembrandt's genre
scenes and depicts a goldsmith at work in his foundry,
gently supporting and completing work at his anvil on the
base of a *caritas* group. The room is lit by the fire at left
and a window at right, articulated in the same masterly,
open, parallel hatching found in *The Golf Player* (cat.
no. 40). This tenderly rendered scene, whose delicacy is
enhanced by subtle light effects (achieved by the drypoint),
by the tenderness of the *caritas* group gently cradled by
the artist, and by the intimacy of the print's dimensions,
was executed in the same year as the artist's portrait *Jan
Lutma, Goldsmith* (cat. nos. 24, 24A) and achieves the
same introspective sensibility as that print. The goldsmith's
pose and gestures eloquently repeat those of the female
caritas figure in an evocative, allegorical intimation of the
creative activity of the artist.

42 Woman Seated Half Dressed Beside a Stove

Date of execution: 1658

Definitive catalogues: H. 296; B., Holl. 197, state III/VII

Process: etching, drypoint, and burin

Data on plate: upper right: Rembrandt f. 1658.

Data on print: on verso, top center: 81 (red pencil); upper left: b (brown ink); 84 (brown ink); lower right center: B.197III H296III (pencil); below preceding: c.28814 (pencil)

Dimensions: 228 mm x 187 mm (8¹⁵⁄₁₆″ x 7⅜″) platemark
230 mm x 190 mm (9¹⁄₁₆″ x 7⁷⁄₁₆″) sheet

Watermarks: undescribed watermark in center with initials IHS

Collections: on verso, lower left corner: L. 1802 [N. Mossoloff, Moscow, 1847–1914]; below preceding: the blue stamp of the Roumiantzoff Museum, Moscow, inv. no. 40571; (Sotheby's, London, December 7, 1983, lot 194)

Rembrandt returned to the theme of the female nude six times in prints between 1658 and 1661. Nudes therefore occupy a prominent position among his late graphic works. Clearly his concerns were not primarily erotic. The woman posed so sculpturally before a stove in a deeply shadowed interior is only slightly idealized and achieves her monumental presence and importance through her relative scale, the soft light that caresses her bared upper torso and head, and the psychological complexity of her reflective expression. The relation of the figure to both the pose and the mood of Rembrandt's 1654 masterpiece, the painting *Bathsheba* (Paris, Louvre), has often been noted. Here, however, the figure is rendered more personal by the domesticity of the tenebrous interior. On the oven door a kneeling figure (the Magdalen?) provides a suggestive complement to the partially nude woman. The somber profile of the stove and chimney, the dark niche against which her head is posed, and the absence of extraneous details (the sheets, chamber pot, and slipper providing the barest personal individuality to the setting) augment the tenor of the contemplative image. The figure's pose is gently animated by the twist of her upper torso and the reciprocal fanning stance of her arms against the head seen in profile.

Rembrandt reworked this print at least seven times, adding drypoint and etched hatching to increase the sculptural definition of the figure and the interior shadow. Although in the first two states the artist focused on the modeling of the woman, in the third state, seen here, he added much shading and definition to the chamber itself. The fourth state is marked by a significant loss of drypoint, the reworking of outline, and the adding of a damper key to the chimney. In the sixth state her cap is removed and her hair revealed coiffed in a bun.

43 Negress Lying Down

Date of execution: 1658

Definitive catalogues: H. 299; B., Holl. 205, state II/III

Process: etching, drypoint, and burin

Data on plate: lower left corner: Rembrandt f. 1658

Data on print: on verso, left center: 202 (pencil); center: B205 (pencil); lower left corner: 12 (pencil)

Dimensions: 83 mm x 158 mm (3¼″ x 6¼″) platemark
90 mm x 167 mm (3⁹⁄₁₆″ x 6⁹⁄₁₆″) sheet

Watermarks: –

Collections: on verso, lower left: RU (brown ink, similar to Lugt 2247, unknown [probably R. Udny, London and Teddington, 1722–1802]); (W. H. Schab, August 23, 1982)

First entitled *Negress Lying Down* by Bartsch, the print is actually a study of the back view of a girl lying in bed in deep shadow. Notably, neither de Jonghe in 1679 (no. 8, "Slaapende naackte vrouwtjes") nor Röver in 1731 ("het slapende vrouwtje") identifies the subject as anything other than a naked sleeping woman. A unique surviving impression of the first state, at the Bibliothèque Nationale, Paris, shows the model significantly paler. The artist decided, however, to darken the shadows throughout and ultimately produced an unforgettable study in shadow and tone. By turning the model away from the viewer he has relied entirely on his mastery of etching and drypoint and the individual inking of each impression to communicate content. Although the overall outline and most of the shading of the legs of the figure were executed in etching, much of the shading of the back and its contours, which dissolve into the enveloping darkness, were created in the richer but far more fleeting medium of drypoint. In the earliest impressions, therefore, the sculptural presence of the female figure softly emerges from the tenebrous background, whereas in weaker impressions the figure seems flat.

The exhibited impression is one of the finest and most brilliant in the world. Richly inked with highlights about the buttocks enhanced by delicate wiping of the plate, this impression appears crisper than fine ones at the Morgan Library and the British Museum (third state), is more richly inked than the second state proof at the Bibliothèque Nationale, and is comparable to the impression at the Metropolitan Museum, New York. This superb example of one of the greatest masterpieces of Rembrandt's career is a triumph of technical accomplishment.

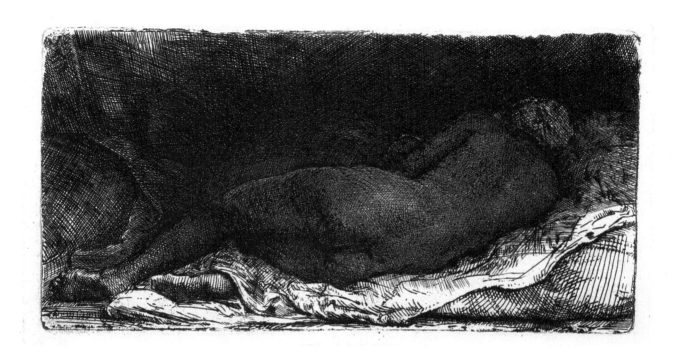

Religious History

44 Presentation in the Temple with the Angel: Small Plate

Date of execution: 1630

Definitive catalogues: H. 18; B., Holl. 51, state II/II

Process: etching and drypoint

Data on plate: in apron, bottom center: RHL (monogram) 1630

Data on print: on recto, lower right corner: 18 (pencil); on verso, upper left corner: 3 (pencil); lower center: B51 (pencil)

Dimensions: 103 mm x 77 mm (4⅟₁₆″ x 3⅟₁₆″) platemark
187 mm x 137 mm (7⅝″ x 5⅝″) sheet

Watermarks: partial, lower portion of a foolscap

Collections: on verso, lower right (almost abraded away): Lugt 2367 [S. S. Scheikevitch, Moscow and Paris, 1842–1908]; (Sotheby's, London, June 14, 1984, lot 147)

In this early version of the *Presentation* the artist's fascination with studies of the elderly and with light and dark contrasts, evident in the contemporary genre studies of 1628–30 (cat. nos. 26–30), are applied to the narration of religious drama. The foreground is established and spatial recession articulated by the repoussoir created by the somewhat confusing figure of the beggar on the far left and the dark ground at the base. The brilliant exterior light, in which the lightly etched contours of the distant architecture and figures dissolve, is contrasted with the shadowed interior of the temple, whose curtained sanctuary is approached by both standing and kneeling figures on a long staircase. The girl at the left looks off toward the beggar and holds the viewer's attention to the foreground.

The confusion of details and the multiplicity of vignettes detract from the coherence and focus of the composition; and the relatively crude use of the etching needle, which contributes little but outlining and shading to the definition of texture and surface, reflects the early date of this work. Yet the conception of the composition as two diagonals, light and dark, interfacing in the foreground where the presentation of the infant Christ takes place, is highly inventive, and the figures of the aged Anna and the gesticulating angel are sensitively drawn.

Figure 15. Lucas van Leyden, *Joseph and the Wife of Potiphar*, engraving, London, British Museum

45 Joseph and Potiphar's Wife

Date of execution: 1634

Definitive catalogues: H. 118; B., Holl. 39, state II/II

Process: etching

Data on plate: bottom left: Rembrandt f. 1634.

Data on print: on verso, top left center: 39 II (pencil); center:
  M.208 (pencil); lower center: U.43 (pencil); bottom right
  center: 75 (pencil)

Dimensions: 91 mm x 115 mm (3⁹⁄₁₆″ x 4⁹⁄₁₆″) platemark
  93 mm x 116 mm (3⅝″ x 4⅝″) sheet

Watermarks: –

Collections: on verso, lower left corner: Lugt 968 [King Ferdinand
  of Portugal, 1816–1885]; below preceding: Lugt 1383 [H.
  Weber, Bonn, 1817–1854]; bottom center: (METZ), stamped
  in black (J. Metz mentioned in Lugt 1109?); (W. H. Schab,
  May 9, 1985)

The story of Joseph and his rejection of the advances of Potiphar's wife is told in Genesis 39.7–12. Rembrandt has chosen to depict the climax of the narrative, when Joseph, struggling to free himself from her embrace, gains the portal by leaving his incriminating cloak in her hands. In this fine, dark, and sensitively inked impression of the highly charged, erotic Biblical theme, Rembrandt effectively uses light and shadow to dramatically oppose the figures, to highlight the nudity and yearning motion of Potiphar's wife (the catalyst of the story), and to spiritually contrast the two figures. The dramatic single diagonal leading the eye to the darkly contoured figure of Joseph and his explicit gesture and motion of rejection as his mantle is pulled from his shoulders, the foreshortening and shading of Joseph's hands, the details of the shadows on the pillows and bedclothes, all reflect Rembrandt's newly gained mastery of composition and technique in the service of a narrative still conceived in Baroque, theatrical terms.

The crudeness with which the nudity of Potiphar's wife is presented, an innovation of the artist, augments the sense of revulsion that we share with Joseph. In fact, her nudity, quite different from the idealized eroticism one finds in Italian depictions, serves to enhance the moralistic impact of the story. When we compare the print to Rembrandt's source, an engraving of over a century earlier by Lucas van Leyden (Bartsch 20, figure 15), we are struck by the dramatic contrast of lighting between the two figures and by the effective use of the nudity of Potiphar's wife in both energizing and morally clarifying the story. How different Rembrandt's communication of naturalistic, feminine nudity can be in a similarly posed figure is immediately evident when Potiphar's wife is compared to the figure of Antiope in the etching of 1631 (cat. no. 31).

46 The Crucifixion: Small Plate

Date of execution: c. 1635

Definitive catalogues: H. 123; B., Holl. 80, state I/I

Process: etching

Data on plate: top center: Rembrandt f.

Data on print: on verso, upper center: 82/9 (pencil); lower
center: fine (pencil); lower right center: ___(?)47 (pencil);
lower left corner:(u)(pencil); bottom right: 501763 (brown ink)

Dimensions: 95 mm x 67 mm (3¾" x 2¹¹⁄₁₆") platemark
95 mm x 68 mm (3¾" x 2¾") sheet

Watermarks: partial, bottom of foolscap (?) with three circles
[see cat. no. 72]

Collections: on verso, lower center: Lugt 1790 (brown ink), "P.
Mariette 1676" [Pierre Mariette II, Paris, 1634–1716]; left
center: Lugt 1220 [G. T. Clough, London, b. 1840]; (Sotheby's,
London, May 15, 1986, lot 64)

The human dimension of the Crucifixion, its emotional
resonance, is effectively expressed in the composition of
this print. The Cross and the static figure of Christ
constitute the physical and psychological fulcrum of a
pyramidal grouping of figures. The eye is guided from the
diagonally foreshortened figure of Christ, at left, down
the Cross to the questioning Magdalen. In the foreground
stands an anonymous spectator, a surrogate for the viewer.
The shaded repoussoir of this central figure, at whom the
Magdalen gazes, establishes the picture plane. From the
poignant, tenderly supported figure of the swooning
Virgin the rotational flow of the composition leads to the
touching gesture of anguish of the delicately shaded
disciple. The eye is held within this group by the figure
of the woman opposite the foreground figure, and the
open, prayerful hands of the disciple guide the viewer back
to the crucified Christ. Each individual is subtly differentiated in his or her response to the divine tragedy,
from the bitter expression of the Pharisee, to the yearning
supplication of the Madonna, to the anonymous figure to
the left of the Cross who covers his face with his hands, lost
in his personal grief. Rembrandt's years of genre studies
are effectively orchestrated in a plaintive and sonorous
harmony of lament.

The present impression is a clear, well-printed image
with notable highlights in such details as the hands
supporting the Virgin and the shadows beneath Christ's
feet.

47 The Tribute Money

Date of execution: c. 1635
Definitive catalogues: H. 124; B., Holl. 68, state I/II
Process: etching
Data on plate: –
Data on print: on verso, upper left corner: G.67 (pencil);
    lower center: B86. (pencil)
Dimensions: 74 mm x 104 mm (2¹⁵⁄₁₆″ x 4⅛″) trimmed to
    platemark
Watermarks: –
Collections: (W. H. Schab, March 16, 1983)

A brilliant, clear impression of the first state, this print depicts the scene recorded in Mark 12.13–17.

And they sent to him some of the Pharisees and some of the Herodians, to entrap him in his talk. And they came and said to him, "Teacher, we know that you are true, and care for no man; for you do not regard the position of men but truly teach the way of God. Is it lawful to pay taxes to Caesar, or not? Should we pay them, or should we not?" But knowing their hypocrisy, he said to them, "Why put me to the test? Bring me a coin, and let me look at it." And they brought one. And he said to them, "Whose likeness and inscription is this?" They said to him, "Caesar's." Jesus said to them, "Render to Caesar the things that are Caesar's, and to God the things that are God's." And they were amazed at him.

As is typical of his work in the 1630s, Rembrandt has chosen to depict the climax of the narrative, as Christ utters his distinction between the temporal and the divine, and has done so in the most dramatic terms. The story provides a marvelous opportunity for the artist to distinguish the various reactions of the Pharisees and Herodians to the pronouncement, and he does this by using light to open up a deep but undistracting space at the left, to focus the viewer's attention on the central arc of figures and the luminous head and critical gesture of Christ, and to reveal the individualized responses of the surrounding figures.

In this relatively early work, Rembrandt still crowds the composition with exotic architectural elements, unrelated episodic details (e.g. the figures at the far left and in the left background), the trappings of rich, brocaded fabrics and oriental costumes, and an unnecessarily large company of figures. The dramatic chiaroscuro therefore functions all the more critically in holding the composition together.

48 The Return of the Prodigal Son

Date of execution: 1636

Definitive catalogues: H. 147; B., Holl. 91, state I/I

Process: etching

Data on plate: lower center on step below figures: Rembrandt
f 1636

Data on print: on recto, lower left corner: 43 (pencil); bottom
right center: W (pencil); on verso, upper left corner: original
(blue pencil); lower center: fine (pencil); lower left corner:
H.147 (pencil); bottom center: 300/_/_ (pencil)

Dimensions: 155 mm x 138 mm (6⅛″ x 5⁷⁄₁₆″) platemark
166 mm x 148 mm (6⁹⁄₁₆″ x 5¹³⁄₁₆″) sheet

Watermarks: –

Collections: (L'Art Ancien, Switzerland, March 22, 1982)

Certainly one of the most touching and universally appealing parables of the Bible, the story of the Prodigal Son (Luke 15.11–32) has been among the most commonly portrayed New Testament themes. Rembrandt turned to it several times, notably in this print of 1636, two drawings (Benesch 562 and 601 [based on Dürer's engraving]), and his last religious painting (Leningrad, Hermitage, c. 1665–68). In that late work the Christian theme of loving forgiveness is interpreted with the most profound simplicity and solemnity; in this version, by contrast, Rembrandt seeks to explore the subject comprehensively as a narrative, interpreting the story with great literalness.

Again, as in cat no. 47, he opens up the space into the distance at left, where the herd from which the fatted calf is to be taken (verse 25) is being tended, while at right a servant brings the robes and shoes requested by the father, and the elder brother looks out reproachfully from behind the portal. The prodigal son's sincere repentance and utter destitution are juxtaposed with the compassion and forgiveness of the father. The foreground steps draw us upward to the central, focal motif of the act of paternal mercy, which is in process before us. The father is seen taking a final step, his rear foot rising out of his sandal, to embrace his son, as the two figures lock into a fixed, architectonic pyramid. The long, arching parallel strokes of the etching needle defining the contours of the father's robe reinforce his protective, enveloping gesture.

The composition itself is directly inspired by a woodcut of the subject by Martin van Heemskerck (Hollstein 53). Rembrandt's 1656 bankruptcy inventory indicates that he owned the graphic corpus of that artist. Despite the number of figures, including such marvelous episodic details as the partially shadowed, curious servant girl, the placement of the figures and their movements and the architectural setting are carefully orchestrated to focus on the central episode of father and son, to far greater effect than in *The Tribute Money* of the previous year (cat. no. 47). This early impression, in fine condition, is beautifully inked and crisply printed.

49 Abraham Caressing Isaac

Date of execution: c. 1637

Definitive catalogues: H. 148; B., Holl. 33, state II/II

Process: etching and drypoint

Data on plate: lower left corner: Rembrandt f.

Data on print: on verso, center: J (pencil); lower right: L- 1023 (?) (pencil); lower left corner: 33 (pencil); bottom center: t (pencil)

Dimensions: 117 mm x 87 mm (4⅝" x 3⁷⁄₁₆") platemark
126 mm x 96 mm (4¹⁵⁄₁₆" x 3¾") sheet

Watermarks: partial, indecipherable

Collections: (Kornfeld und Klipstein, Bern, auction 179, June 26, 1981, lot 157)

In this touching work drawn with rapid strokes and a sensitive range of deepening tone from right to left, the artist conceives of the poignant relation between the patriarch and the beloved child of his old age as much in terms of a colloquy of hands as in terms of expressions. The wildflowers and the shadows subtly frame the figures, which are presented with informal directness and utmost authenticity of feeling.

The print marks a noteworthy shift in Rembrandt's narrative concerns. Abjuring the clear and melodramatic gestures and passions of his earlier work, he presents figures of far greater psychological complexity in less purely illustrative narrative depictions. The richness of experience and the mystery of divine dispensation underlying Abraham's relation to his son are intimated rather than expressly depicted in his enigmatic expression and caressing hands. The artist complementarily relies on a middle range of light and shadow rather than the brilliant contrasts of chiaroscuro typical of his earlier work.

50 Abraham Casting Out Hagar and Ishmael

Date of execution: 1637

Definitive catalogues: H. 149; B., Holl. 30, state I/I

Process: etching and drypoint

Data on plate: upper right corner: Rembrandt f 1637

Data on print: on verso, lower left center: B.30 (pencil); lower
 right: c.644 (pencil); bottom center: 19 (pencil)

Dimensions: 126 mm x 96 mm (4¹⁵⁄₁₆" x 3¾") platemark
 133 mm x 102 mm (5¼" x 4") sheet

Watermarks: large double-headed eagle with crown

Collections: on verso, lower left corner: Lugt 1110a [J. G.
 Guildal, Copenhagen, 1855–1920]; (Sotheby's, London, June
 27, 1985, lot 368)

The richly anecdotal presentation of this story has
ensured its enduring popularity. Hollstein (White, Boon)
records no fewer than ten printed copies after it. The
impression presented is an early one, with drypoint still
visible along the contour of Abraham's turban. Among
the most engaging narrative details are the figure of the
young Isaac emerging from the shadows to peek out at the
expulsion of Hagar and his stepbrother, and the bitter
smile of the aged Sarah as she watches the tearful departure
of her rival. With complete mastery of his medium, the
artist suggests the varying textures of the patriarch's exotic
robes and furs. The central figure of Abraham, caught
between his two families at the moment of compelled
choice, is placed pivotally in the composition, his gestures
explicit and poignant.

51 The Triumph of Mordecai

Date of execution: c. 1641

Definitive catalogues: H. 172; B., Holl. 40, state I/I

Process: etching and drypoint

Data on plate: –

Data on print: on verso, upper right: ④917B (vertical in pencil); center: 6620 Pett___(?) (diagonally in pencil); lower right edge: 6020___(?) (vertical in pencil); lower left: 6 (upside down in pencil); base center: HΘ (pencil)

Dimensions: 175 mm x 215 mm (6⅞″ x 8⁷⁄₁₆″) trimmed to platemark

Watermarks: –

Collections: on verso, top center: Lugt 2133 (black ink), "T. Rechberger 1803" [T. Rechberger, Vienna, 1771–1841]; below preceding: Lugt 2897 [E. Smith, Jr., London, second half 19th c.]; lower left center: des collections Fries et Verstolk (below the underlined portion of the preceding appear the letters MEP; all in pencil); (Christie's, New York, May 2, 1980, lot 98); (Sotheby Parke Bernet, New York, November 13, 1980, private sale 1063593)

  Note: On Baron J. G. Verstolk van Soelen (1776–1845) see Lugt 2490. The preceding inscription is consistent with the fact that the lot of five volumes containing the work of Rembrandt and his school in the Fries sale, Amsterdam, June 1824, was sold to Brondgeest, as Lugt notes, "probablement pour le baron Verstolk" (see Lugt 2903). Of the Verstolk collection, Lugt notes, "Son oeuvre de Rembrandt était un des plus beaux jamais rassemblés." Rechberger was the keeper of the Count Moriz von Fries (Lugt 2903) collection until c. 1820, when he became Curator of the Albertina, Vienna.

The story of the triumphal procession of Mordecai, a Jew who had saved the life of the Persian king Ahasuerus, is recorded in Esther 6.1–11. Mordecai is led in royal robes and on the king's steed through the streets of Susa by the mortified royal counselor Haman, who was planning the annihilation of the Jews. The double irony of the story derives from the fact that, when asked by the king what should be done for one he chose to honor, Haman, assuming that Ahasuerus meant him, had suggested this

Figure 16. Lucas van Leyden, *The Triumph of Mordecai*, engraving, London, British Museum

tribute. Rembrandt returned to the story of Esther on several occasions throughout his career, depicting different episodes (see cat. no. 10).

The composition is itself a triumph of the integration of figures, architecture, and the media of etching and drypoint to present a single, focused episode, and anticipates the artist's achievement a year later in the complex painted portrait group of *The Night Watch (The Company of Captain Frans Banning Cocq)*. As in that work, light plays a prominent role by brilliantly illuminating the foreground figures against a shadowed middle ground and a sketchily defined distance. The artist has added the charming detail, not found in the text, of King Ahasuerus and Queen Esther regarding the event from the royal porch. These figures have been recognized as slightly idealized portraits of Rembrandt and his wife, Saskia. Rembrandt has also intensified the sensation of processional movement by compelling the viewer to read the print from right to left. This orientation is not an accident of the compositional transfer process of printmaking, since he uses the same device in *The Night Watch*. The figures in the crowd were based on life studies, at least one of which survives (Benesch 732). The action of the crowd is contrasted with the solemn dignity of Mordecai, whose nobility is augmented by the architectural setting.

Rembrandt, who owned prints by Lucas van Leyden, was certainly aware of his engraving of the subject (Bartsch 32, figure 16), to which his own print is clearly indebted, both in overall composition and in figural details. In Lucas's print, however, the figures are in rapid, uninterrupted motion from left to right. As Christopher White has noted, Rembrandt, by changing the directionality of the march and setting the figures of Mordecai and Haman before a monumental, enframing arch, and through Haman's gestures, clearly has chosen to depict the moment in which Haman, stopping the march, must proclaim, "This shall be done to the one whom the king delights to honor" (verse 11). The humiliation of Haman is augmented by the presence of the king and queen; thus Rembrandt's self-introduction with Saskia is not merely anecdotal, but enhances and underlines the meaning of the story.

One of the most brilliant impressions in the entire Weil Rembrandt collection, this print exemplifies the extraordinary use of drypoint in an early impression. It is exceptionally rich in inking, especially at the lower left (e.g. the kneeling man) and in details on the right side (e.g. the child kneeling behind the dogs). Selective toning of the print with thin films of ink left on the plate has been accomplished in a subtle and masterly manner, notably in the figures behind the horse and the porch shadows. Drypoint no longer serves simply to accent details; rather, its effects are integrated in the overall conception of the print's execution. It is used not only to shadow the figures at left, but also to draw many of the figures, so that its richly burred subtleties make an early impression all the more important to the aesthetic appreciation of the work. To complete such a composition in its final form in a single state is an amazing accomplishment.

52 Christ Crucified Between Two Thieves: An Oval Plate

Date of execution: c. 1641

Definitive catalogues: H. 173; B., Holl. 79, state I/II

Process: etching and drypoint

Data on plate: –

Data on print: – The print is mounted. On verso of old mount, upper left center: 1 etat (pencil); center: 12P (pencil); below preceding: B79iRI (an2) SI (an3) H1731 (an2 + 2) Mz 215I (an2) BB41_2I (an2) (all in pencil); lower right center: 305 (pencil)

Dimensions: 132 mm x 98 mm (5⅛" x 3⅞") platemark
148 mm x 110 mm (5¹³⁄₁₆" x 4⁵⁄₁₆") sheet

Watermarks: mounted

Collections: on verso, lower right center: Lugt 1138c [G. Biörklund, Stockholm, b. 1887]; center: AW (pencil) [Adolph Weil, Jr., Montgomery, Alabama]; (Wechsler, n.d.)

The *Christ Crucified Between Two Thieves* constitutes a remarkable advance in the multivalent communication of content over the version of the Crucifixion created only six years earlier (cat. no. 46). Although the compositions are similar, Rembrandt here has conveyed not only the personal but also the spiritual significance of the event, drawing on all the technical skills he had mastered in the intervening years. A mystical light seems to emanate from the body of Christ, and his Cross dominates the composition, rising upward toward the heavens in a powerful vertical that suggests far more the conviction of triumph than the finality of death. In the half-shadows beneath, the brooding human figures and the bowed horse, in a responding counterpoint, express in simple, natural, and untheatrical gestures the personal grief and anguish attending His sacrifice. The advance in Rembrandt's empathetic subtlety of expression over the 1635 print is profound. The placement of the figures and the oval format of the composition tenderly frame Christ's looming, luminous profile.

53 Three Oriental Figures (Jacob and Laban?)

Date of execution: 1641
Definitive catalogues: H. 183; B., Holl. 118, state II/II
Process: etching
Data on plate: upper right corner: Rembrandt f 1641 (reversed)
Data on print: –
Dimensions: 145 mm x 114 mm (5¾" x 4½") platemark
146 mm x 114 mm (5¾" x 4½") trimmed to
platemark on top, left and right, thread margin
at bottom
Watermarks: –
Collections: on verso, lower left corner: AW (pencil) [Adolph
Weil, Jr., Montgomery, Alabama]; (Sotheby Parke Bernet,
New York, May 12, 1972, lot 615)

As Hind notes, the title *Jacob and Laban* was first
suggested in the nineteenth century by Charles Blanc
(*L'Oeuvre complet de Rembrandt décrit et commenté*,
2 vols., Paris, 1859–61, cat. no. 7) and Charles Henry
Middleton (*Descriptive Catalogue of the Etched Work of
Rembrandt van Rhyn*, London, 1878, cat. no. 212). Hind
adopted that title with reservations. Earlier, Bartsch (1797)
had simply entitled the work *Three Oriental Figures*.
Since the print does not clearly relate to any episode in
the story of Jacob and Laban (Genesis 29–31), and since
such ambiguity in the depiction of religious histories was
not Rembrandt's practice, Bartsch's title is probably more
accurate. However, the assumption that the print is a
simple genre scene, like, for example, the contemporary
Woman at a Door Hatch Talking to a Man and Children
(B., Holl. 128), is not entirely satisfying, given the
specific setting and oriental costumes. It is possible that
the etching illustrates a play or story whose subject we
do not know. Rembrandt created several such illustrational
prints, including two in this same year (B., Holl. 120
and 148).

The artist's stylistic progression in the early 1640s toward
simpler, less episodic and detailed compositions and his
use of a looser, more open drawing technique, creating
the effect of light and atmosphere through the luminosity
of the paper itself, are strikingly clear if one compares
this print with the similarly set *Abraham Casting Out
Hagar and Ishmael* (cat. no. 50) of only four years earlier.

54   The Raising of Lazarus: Small Plate

Date of execution: 1642

Definitive catalogues: H. 198; B., Holl. 72, state I/II

Process: etching

Data on plate: lower left corner: Rembrandt f 1642 (2 reversed)

Data on print: on verso, lower left corner: N___(?) (pencil);
   below preceding: 72 (pencil)

Dimensions: 150 mm x 115 mm (5⅞" x 4⅞") platemark
              163 mm x 128 mm (6⁷⁄₁₆" x 5¹⁄₁₆") sheet

Watermarks: –

Collections: on verso, lower center: Lugt 654 [P. Davidsohn,
   Grunewald-Berlin, b. 1839]; lower left center: Lugt 33 [August
   Artaria, Vienna, 1807–1893]; (Sotheby's, New York, November
   8, 1984, lot 42)

Figure 17. Rembrandt, *The Raising of Lazarus: The Larger Plate,* etching and burin, state III/X, Paris, Bibliothèque Nationale

Rembrandt previously had portrayed the miracle of the raising of Lazarus in a print of 1632 (B., Holl. 73, figure 17). That etching presents the event far more majestically and theatrically but with far less authentic spirituality. Indeed, the stylistic and iconographic differences between the two versions are remarkable. The 1632 print is a consummate example of Rembrandt's early approach to religious history. In an exotic setting with dramatic chiaroscuro, the immense, looming, profiled figure of Christ, set diagonally into space, his face turned from the viewer, summons Lazarus from the grave through the imperious and highly dramatic gesture of his raised hand, brightly lit against the dark stone wall. Theatrically the attendant figures, set in space to reinforce the diagonal sweep of the composition, react to the astounding miracle.

As White has noted, Rembrandt returned in a preparatory drawing for this 1642 print (Benesch 518) to the Jan Lievens etching (c. 1630, B. 3) that had inspired the first version. Ultimately, however, a more human and accessible Christ is further integrated into the crowd and the miracle acquires the poignancy of an intimately experienced event (the etching plate is one-fifth the size of the 1632 print). Abjuring obvious dramatic devices, Rembrandt renders the resurrection as a highly mystical and personal experience. Lazarus mysteriously and pathetically is drawn out from the grave, the febrile strokes of the etching needle barely defining him against the white stone wall, as, isolated on the right half of the composition, he is called forth less by the gesture of Christ than by the spiritual evocation of his prayers. Jesus stands out from his context by the whiteness of his robes against the softly shaded background and by the verticality of his pose. The figures about him respond with fright and wonder, but without the theatricality of the 1632 version. The focus of the print is the personal colloquy between Christ and the resurrected Lazarus.

As in the *Triumph of Mordecai* (cat. no. 51), the shading, the archway, and the attendant figures frame the brightly lit protagonists. The present fine and early impression of the first state reveals the subtle manner in which Rembrandt has reinforced the contour of Christ's upper body to further isolate him. Accents are also visible in the shadows of the kneeling woman in the left foreground (Martha?) and along the head of Lazarus. These effects, which serve both spatial and thematic concerns of the artist, are rapidly lost in the second state.

55 Abraham and Isaac

Date of execution: 1645
Definitive catalogues: H. 214; B., Holl. 34, state I/I
Process: etching and drypoint
Data on plate: lower left corner: Rembrandt. 1645.
Data on print: on recto, bottom left: awb (?) (black ink); on verso, upper left: n (brown ink); lower center: H. 214 (pencil); lower left corner: C.U.T. (pencil); 45175 (pencil)
Dimensions: 157 mm x 130 mm (6¼₆″ x 5⅛″) platemark
158 mm x 130 mm (6⅛″ x 5⅛″) sheet trimmed to platemark with thread margins, trimmed just within margin on left

Watermarks: –

Collections: on recto, upper right corner: Lugt 2849 [G. Hibbert, London, 1757–1837]; on verso, lower center: James Coll. (pencil); lower left corner: AW (pencil) [Adolph Weil, Jr., Montgomery, Alabama]; (Sotheby Parke Bernet, New York, May 8, 1975, lot 539)

Figure 18. Rembrandt, *Abraham's Sacrifice*, red and black chalk, wash in India ink, heightened with white gouache, on greenish-yellow paper, London, British Museum

The story of the sacrifice of Abraham appears in Genesis 22.1–19; in this etching the artist depicts the episode described in verses 6–8.

And Abraham took the wood of the burnt offering, and laid it on Isaac his son; and he took in his hand the fire and the knife. So they went both of them together. And Isaac said to his father Abraham, "My father!" And he said, "Here am I, my son." He said, "Behold the fire and the wood: but where is the lamb for a burnt offering?" Abraham said, "God will provide himself the lamb for a burnt offering, my son." So they went both of them together.

Extraordinarily, Rembrandt chooses not to depict the actual act of sacrifice, a traditional theme that had been the subject of his highly theatrical 1635 painting (Leningrad, Hermitage; preparatory drawing, London, British Museum, Benesch 90, figure 18), to focus on an earlier moment of personal dialogue, when Abraham, caught between his paternal love and spiritual obedience, confronts his son, who gazes at him with total filial trust. Rembrandt achieves with moving directness and eloquent simplicity the expression of a highly complex and profound human experience.

From about 1640 a shift from a more ostentatious, forceful, explicit, and physical depiction of religious narrative to an emphasis on internal spiritual values, and in this work on the inner conflicts that confront man in his obedience to a transcendent God, characterizes Rembrandt's religious art. Abraham's raised hand both gestures his son forward and points to the Divine source of sacrifice, while his other hand unconsciously draws to his chest, expressing his inner torment. The innocent Isaac studies the pregnant gesture of his father. Indeed, the hand is the poignant focus of both figures' concentration and the key to the meaning of the work. How much more subtle and yet emotionally wrenching this depiction of a quiet moment of spiritual crisis is than such dramatically explicit works of the previous decade as cat. nos. 45, 47, and 48!

The figures, whose contours are reinforced in drypoint and whose shading is drawn in an elaborate network of short, fine hatching strokes, stand in virtual sculptural relief from the landscape, which is sketchily defined in long, rapidly drawn parallel lines. This stylistic innovation was inspired by the engravings of Mantegna, whose early Renaissance prints Rembrandt began studying at this time (see comments, cat. no. 61).

56 St. Jerome Beside a Pollard Willow

Date of execution: 1648
Definitive catalogues: H. 232; B., Holl. 103, state II/II
Process: etching, drypoint, and burin
Data on plate: bottom center: Rembrandt f.1648
Data on print: on verso, bottom center: Nr.103.II (pencil);
    below preceding: 25213 (pencil)
Dimensions: 177 mm x 131 mm (6¹⁵⁄₁₆″ x 5³⁄₁₆″) platemark
    181 mm x 135 mm (7⅛″ x 5⁵⁄₁₆″) sheet
Watermarks: –
Collections: on verso, lower left corner: Lugt 660 [Charles
    Delanglade, Marseilles, b. 1870]; (Sotheby's, London, July 9,
    1985, lot 391)

St. Jerome appears in seven etchings by Rembrandt, and
is the only doctor of the Church the artist portrayed. In
this print, one of Rembrandt's most endearing owing to
the charm of the impersonal presentation of the subject,
the saint is placed outdoors, seated on a bench, his
cardinal's hat propped beside him and his companion
lion peacefully looking out at the landscape, as he works
on his translation of the Scripture, his eyeglasses perched
on his nose. Hardly the irascible, aloof scholar and hieratic
doctor of the Church traditionally portrayed, Rembrandt's
figure is that of the gentle hermit at work, a humanist at
peace with nature.

Only the pollard willow has been worked up in detail.
The mighty, central trunk has been carefully drawn in
etching; the figures of the saint and the lion and the
surrounding landscape details are added in drypoint. A
surviving, beautifully rendered study of the trunk (Turin,
Library, Benesch 852a), drawn from nature, would seem
to confirm that the etching plate was first worked up as a
study of the massive and lovingly described gnarled tree,
to which the other elements were then added. In the final
composition, the saint, absorbed in his work, seems
immured within his natural isolation. Enclosing cliffs and
a waterfall are barely suggested in the most summary
strokes of drypoint. The tree itself serves both as a compositional foil and as a natural complement to the figure
of the saint. Both aged and characterful, the weather-
beaten, nearly lifeless willow sends out a lush young shoot,
added in drypoint, which both shelters and frames the
saint, affirming the vitality of his activity despite his
physical mortality (expressed by the skull).

The rich drypoint work is contrasted with the open
space of the design, permitting the paper to evoke the
brilliance of a summer day. The added details of burin in
the second state, shading the foreground grasses and the
earth beneath the saint's feet along the riverbank and
creating a transition between the deep, velvety lines of
drypoint and the delicacy of etching, are evidence of
the artist's mastery in integrating techniques.

Although Dürer's drypoint of St. Jerome (Bartsch 59)
has been suggested as a source for the composition, I would
propose that Rembrandt was inspired by two closely

Figure 19. Marcantonio Raimondi, *St. Jerome*, engraving,
London, British Museum

Figure 20. Marcantonio Raimondi, *St. Jerome and the Small
Lion*, engraving, London, British Museum

related early engravings by Marcantonio Raimondi
(Bartsch 101, figure 19; and Bartsch 102, figure 20, after
a design by Titian). Rembrandt owned and studied
engravings by Marcantonio and a book of prints after
Titian (see comments, cat. nos. 57, 58, and 68); and
indeed there is a Venetian influence both in the informality
of the depiction and in the natural setting that dominates
the composition and establishes its tenor.

57 The Blindness of Tobit: The Larger Plate

Date of execution: 1651
Definitive catalogues: H. 252; B., Holl. 42, state I/II
Process: etching and drypoint
Data on plate: bottom center right: Rembrandt f 1651; lower
    right corner: Rembrandt f 1651
Data on print: on verso, top center: D (brown ink); lower right:
    40 (pencil)
Dimensions: 162 mm x 128 mm (6⅜″ x 5¹⁄₁₆″) platemark
             166 mm x 131 mm (6½″ x 5³⁄₁₆″) sheet
Watermarks: –
Collections: on verso, lower left corner: Lugt 176 [H. Danby
    Seymour, London and Trent, 1820–1877]; (Sotheby Parke
    Bernet, New York, November 19, 1982, lot 556)

The story of Tobit, as told in the Apocrypha, fascinated Rembrandt: he devoted five paintings, three etchings, and 36 surviving drawings to the subject. The episode depicted here is that recounted in Apocrypha, Tobit 11.10, when the old, blind man, hearing the approach of his son, for whose return he had been anxiously waiting, rises to meet him. In this mature work the artist has treated the theme of blindness with great compassion and intimacy, placing the figure in a simple domestic interior with such personalizing details as the fish hanging in the fireplace and the spinning wheel overturned by the old man. Tobit's faltering motion toward the door and his misdirection, emphasized by the shadow cast on the wall, are touchingly underlined by the action of his dog, which attempts to guide his master after he has been disoriented by the fallen wheel. Through the simplest of technical means, broadly spaced parallel hatchings and broad blank fields, the artist has isolated the brightly lit figure of the blind man and his shadow.

It was Blanc (1859–61, no. 15) who first noted that the figure of the blind Tobit echoes that of Elymas in the tapestry cartoon *The Blinding of Elymas*, which Rembrandt could have studied in the 1516 engraving of Agostino Veneziano (Bartsch 43, the figure reversed in Rembrandt's print). The artist's inventory of 1656 records several books of engravings after Raphael (items 196, 205, 206, 214). The shaded foreground sets the figure on a subtly raised stage. As in *The Triumph of Mordecai* (cat. no. 51), the uncommon orientation of the composition from right to left augments the sense of the motion of the central figure, here the hesitant, unsure steps of the blind Tobit.

58 Christ Preaching ('La Petite Tombe')

Date of execution: c. 1652
Definitive catalogues: H. 256; B., Holl. 67, state I/I
Process: etching, drypoint, and burin
Data on plate: –
Data on print: (mounted on all four corners on hand-laid paper; on mount, recto, lower right: good impression and rare [pencil])
Dimensions: 155 mm x 207 mm (6⅛″ x 8⅛″) trimmed to platemark
Watermarks: foolscap
Collections: (Christie's, London, June 24, 1986, lot 269)

This image of *Christ Preaching* has been known as *La Petite Tombe* since 1751, when Gersaint so titled it, based on a misunderstanding of Clement de Jonghe's 1679 inventory. In the earlier compilation the work was listed as "Latombisch plaatjens," which more accurately translates as "the little print of la Tombe." Rembrandt probably created the etching for a friend, the art dealer Pieter de la Tombe. Gersaint misread the title and interpreted the block on which Christ stands as a tomb. As early as 1756, Pierre Yver, in his supplement to Gersaint's catalogue, noted the likelihood of such a confusion, but Gersaint's title endured.

The composition is based on Raphael's *Parnassus* in the Vatican, Stanza della Segnatura, which Rembrandt would have known through Marcantonio Raimondi's engraving (Bartsch 247, figure 21; on Rembrandt's extensive collection of prints after Raphael, see cat. no. 57). The head and upper torso of Christ are derived from the seated Christ in Raphael's *Disputa*, in the same chamber at the Vatican, which was also accessible to him through prints. In the same year, in a dated drawing given to his friend Jan Six, Rembrandt based a very similar composition (*Homer Reciting*, Benesch 913) even more explicitly on the *Parnassus*. Several figures in the drawing were reused in the figures grouped around Christ in the print.

As in *The Hundred Guilder Print* of c. 1649 (B., Holl. 74, figure 22) the work presents Christ preaching to the public, but unlike that earlier print, in which the artist has synthesized the activities and teachings of several different verses from Matthew 19, this simpler, reserved composition contains no specific reference to any verse. Rather, the subject seems to be the very compassionate message of *agape*—selfless love itself. It is as if the artist has sought to visualize not a physical event but the very essence of human values at the heart of Christ's teachings, to depict physically in a scene of utmost intimacy the most exalted and spiritual of human experiences.

To convey this theme, Rembrandt has relied on a far simpler compositional structure than that of *The Hundred Guilder Print*. The figures are set in a small courtyard

Figure 21. Marcantonio Raimondi, *Parnassus*, engraving, London, British Museum

Figure 22. Rembrandt, *The Hundred Guilder Print*, etching, drypoint, and burin, state II/II, Cambridge, Massachusetts, Fogg Art Museum (Harvard University Art Museums)

that opens to the outside world through a simple portal at right. How different this setting is from the grand space and monumental gateway in the earlier work! The figure of Christ is no longer distinguished by greater physical stature, but is set at the center of a circular assembly of auditors, who respond to his teachings by quiet meditation. The moral force and meaning of his words and gestures hold the assembly by a spiritual power, as though the figures have become satellites held in position about the brilliantly lit figure of Christ. The light seems to emanate from within Jesus, radiating outwards, one powerful burst of spiritual light rising toward (and descending from) the heavens.

Each of the figures is absorbed in the most personal and individualized of meditations upon the words of Christ. Deliberative poses and gestures, at once inimitable yet universal, are given to such figures as the youth in half-shadow at Christ's left and the old man, his hand to his mouth, lost in reflection. Even the child drawing on the ground is caught within the tenor and mood of the scene, and his form locks into the circle about Christ. Christ is placed centrally in this most sober of compositions; the vertical shaft of light reinforces that central axis, and the base of the podium on which he stands is visible through the humanity about him as an arc shape, both isolating him and completing the circular pattern framing him. The shadows that serve to isolate the brightly lit Christ and emphasize his spirituality also express the impact of his message. Christ's pose and balanced gestures, the architectural setting, and the disposition of the figures about him lend a classical structure and symmetry to the work, which is typical of Rembrandt's style in the 1650s.

Rembrandt's drawing style is also simpler than in *The Hundred Guilder Print.* He uses a far more open system of hatching strokes, with a repeated pattern of vertical and horizontal lines that complements the stable organization of the composition. The initial drawing of the figures was executed in etching, and the work was completed in drypoint and burin. The drypoint not only enriches the shadows and velvety surfaces, but also contributes to the mysterious, tender, tenebrous mood of the print. Thus the finest impressions of this print tend to be the most richly inked early impressions. The present impression is an extraordinarily rich and brilliant one, with unusually dark, glistening ink passages in the robes of the standing figure at the far left and in Christ's robes. The black sleeve of the left figure's right arm appears white in later impressions, and formed the basis of the distinction applied more generally in differentiating Rembrandt's inkings of his mature prints between "white-sleeve" (the Dutch expression being "met het witte mouwtje") and heavily inked "black-sleeve" impressions. The Weil impression is comparable in quality to the finest British Museum black-sleeve impression.

59 The Adoration of the Shepherds: With the Lamp

Date of execution: c. 1654

Definitive catalogues: H. 273; B., Holl. 45, state I/II

Process: etching

Data on plate: bottom left center: Rembrandt f.

Data on print: on verso, vertically along left edge at top: ger.44 (pencil); center: B45I (pencil); H274I (pencil); c.26854 (pencil); vertically along lower left edge: Marse a/y_ (pencil); bottom left corner: 3300 a.f.a. (pencil)

Dimensions: 105 mm x 130 mm (4⅛″ x 5⅛″) platemark
109 mm x 133 mm (4¼″ x 5³⁄₁₆″) sheet

Watermarks: partial foolscap

Collections: (Sotheby Parke Bernet, New York, November 14, 1981, lot 825)

The intimacy and warmth of the tender, hesitant responses of the simple shepherds and attending peasants to the Infant are augmented by their circular compositional grouping about the adored Madonna and Child, a device used in *Christ Preaching* (cat. no. 58). Joseph's welcoming gesture encloses the circle, urging the figures at left forward and down the steps. The lighting in this work, which functions much as in *Christ Preaching* to isolate and communicate the spiritual exaltedness of the central figures, is supplied by a small lamp set against the wall. The artist has placed the scene in a simple stable, the Child resting, as the Bible describes, in a humble manger, while to the right two gentle bulls enclose the composition. The scene is one of utter domesticity and disarming parental pride. Rubens had set the Holy Family in a similarly lit arch in his painting *The Adoration of the Shepherds* (Marseilles, Musée des Beaux-Arts), which Rembrandt could have known from a print.

About 1654 the artist created six small prints, all of approximately the same proportions and size, on subjects related to the infancy and youth of Christ, four of which are represented in the Weil collection (cat. nos. 59–62). This is a fine, darkly and cleanly inked impression of the first of two states, with the open, parallel hatching strokes of the artist's later style.

60 The Circumcision in the Stable

Date of execution: 1654

Definitive catalogues: H. 274; B., Holl. 47, state I/II

Process: etching

Data on plate: upper left corner: Rembrandt f 1654 (a and d reversed); center at left margin: Rembrandt f 1654

Data on print: on verso, center: H 4_(?) (pencil); lower center: 8326 (pencil); lower right: B 43I (pencil); below preceding: Kais 285 (pencil); lower left corner: CD#10 (pencil)

Dimensions: 94 mm x 144 mm (3¾″ x 5¹¹⁄₁₆″) platemark
96 mm x 147 mm (3¹³⁄₁₆″ x 5¾″) sheet

Watermarks: indecipherable

Collections: on verso, lower left: Lugt 1041c [F. Quiring, Berlin, b. 1886]; Lugt 1681ter [Dr. F. A. Lieberg, Buenos Aires, b. 1898]; above preceding: AW (pencil) [Adolph Weil, Jr., Montgomery, Alabama]; (Karl und Faber, Munich, auction 131, December 2, 1972, lot 165)

The Circumcision in the Stable is another in the series of small etchings of 1654 depicting in intimate domesticity the infancy and youth of Christ (see cat. nos. 59 and 61–62). The focal figures, isolated by a descending light at once natural and supernatural, are absorbed in their responses to the event. Joseph carefully holds the Infant securely, while the nurse looks on with interest and Mary demurely looks aside from the illuminated, sacramental hands of the circumciser.

Interestingly, Rembrandt has set the scene not in the Temple, but in a stable. The Bible (Luke 2.21) simply states, "And at the end of eight days, when he was circumcised he was called Jesus, the name given by the angel before he was conceived in the womb." According to Mosaic law, Mary could not have entered the Temple until the period of ritual purification after birth, 40 days, was completed. The traditional localizing of the Circumcision in the Temple in Western art perhaps derived from a conflation with representations of the Presentation (see cat. no. 44).

In the 1640s and 1650s Rembrandt's close personal contacts with leading members and scholars of the Jewish community (see cat. nos. 13 and 21; his mansion on Breestraat was adjacent to the Jewish quarter) may well have acquainted him with such traditional errors of representation, including some that he himself had previously committed (e.g. *The Circumcision: Small Plate*, c. 1630, B., Holl. 48). Setting the action in the stable, however, rather than in the grand and monumental Temple, also helped the artist to achieve the simplicity and intimacy we find in all the prints in this series. Traces of acid corrosion and sulfur tint in the plate contribute to the warm tonality and palpable atmosphere (see technical comments, cat. nos. 18 and 66).

Figure 23. Andrea Mantegna, *The Virgin and Child*, engraving, London, British Museum

61 The Virgin and Child with the Cat and Snake

Date of execution: 1654

Definitive catalogues: H. 275; B., Holl. 63, state I/II

Process: etching

Data on plate: bottom center: Rembrandt. f. 1654.

Data on print: on verso, lower right center: T Abonate (?) (pencil); below preceding: No 341 (pencil); bottom center: $ABev/st3 Died agr (pencil); bottom left center: <u>c7216</u> (pencil); lower left corner: (crossed out) E1590 (pencil)

Dimensions: 96 mm x 144 mm (3¾" x 5¹¹⁄₁₆") platemark
 102 mm x 156 mm (4" x 6³⁄₁₆") sheet

Watermarks: –

Collections: (Christie's, New York, May 3, 1983, lot 535)

This print, another of the series of small etchings of 1654 dealing with the infancy of Christ, turns directly to an engraving by Mantegna for its source (*The Virgin and Child*, Hind 5.10.1, figure 23). Rembrandt admired the Quattrocento master. His 1656 inventory records " 't kostelijcke boek van Andre de Mantaingie" (no. 200, the precious volume of Andrea Mantegna). During the same period on two other occasions he copied Mantegna's work in pen-and-ink drawings (Benesch 1207, c. 1656, a copy of the Mantegna [school] drawing of the *Calumny of Apelles*; Benesch 105a, a copy of the engraving *The Entombment* [an attributed drawing, if not from his own hand, clearly from his studio]).

In the cited works Rembrandt seems particularly concerned with capturing Mantegna's linear style, and, as has been noted, this open, parallel hatching style that defines figures in sculptural relief from their background appears in other works of the period (e.g. cat. nos. 40 and 58). Rembrandt's modifications of Mantegna's Virgin and Child group, however, are as interesting as his borrowings. Softening and simplifying the crisp, Gothic folds of the Virgin's dress, attiring her in more modern clothing, placing her in a contemporary, charming, and humble domestic interior, raising the viewpoint, he makes the figures seem softer and more accessible, less hieratic and sculpturesque. Although they face away from the light, Rembrandt frames them in light from the window, whose rectilinearity is gently broken by the delightful device of Joseph peering inside. Thus the entire Holy Family is set in light as a group.

While adopting the Italian master's manner of parallel hatching, Rembrandt constantly shifts the angle of his linear network, animating the composition and modulating the interior shadows. He also introduces into this quiet, humble domestic scene the traditional iconographic note of the serpent crushed beneath the foot of Mary (the new Eve), a symbol of the victory of Christ's Incarnation over Satan.

62 Christ Seated Disputing with the Doctors

Date of execution: 1654

Definitive catalogues: H. 277; B., Holl. 64, state I/I

Process: etching

Data on plate: top left center: Rembrandt.f.1654.

Data on print: on recto, upper left corner: R. 68(?) (pencil); on verso, upper left corner: Gerst No 63 (pencil); upper right corner: B_(?) GE (pencil)

Dimensions: 95 mm x 144 mm (3¾″ x 5⅝″) platemark
113 mm x 161 mm (4½″ x 6⅜″) sheet

Watermarks: –

Collections: on verso, lower left corner: purple collection stamp of Felix Somary (Vienna and Zurich, 1881–1956); (N. G. Stogdon, Somary Sale, cat. no. 12, November 14, 1985)

This etching is one of six in a group of small prints designed in 1654 and related to the infancy and youth of Christ, four of which are in the Weil collection (see cat. nos. 59–61). The charm of this composition, drawn in open, parallel strokes that create a sense of airiness, rests in the informality of the moment. The youthful Christ rocks his right leg as he gestures in a moment of animated discussion with a doctor seated astride a long bench. Figures gather around out of intellectual interest (e.g. the standing figure unselfconsciously pulling on a strand of his beard as he ponders) or sheer curiosity (e.g. the leaning elder at right).

In a preparatory sketch, in reverse, at the National-museum in Stockholm (Benesch 936), the figures, including a smaller, younger, and deferentially posed Jesus, are presented in a colonnaded interior with an arch opening up on the left to what appears to be a grand stairway, from which two figures are rising into view. In the print the figures are enlarged in relative scale to their setting and brought forward, especially Jesus, who now commands the scene; the interior is simplified and less grandiose; and the stairway space is replaced by the balcony over which the picturesque group of elders stare and brood. Although the tall foreground figure has been kept, his long robes in the drawing have been replaced by more contemporary and far less exalted attire, and the beard has been added. In summary, the artist has again rejected a more traditional and hieratic depiction in favor of one of great directness and experiential accessibility.

63 Abraham's Sacrifice

Date of execution: 1655

Definitive catalogues: H. 283; B., Holl. 35, state I/I

Process: etching and drypoint

Data on plate: bottom right: Rembrandt f 1655 (d and 6 reversed)

Data on print: on verso, top center: HG (brown ink); upper
   center: No. 39 (brown ink); upper right corner: 33 (brown ink)

Dimensions: 156 mm x 132 mm (6⅛″ x 5¼″) platemark
          158 mm x 133 mm (6³⁄₁₆″ x 5³⁄₁₆″) sheet

Watermarks: –

Collections: (Sotheby Parke Bernet, New York, February 15,
   1980, lot 1028)

The print portrays Abraham's tragic moment of sacrifice
and miraculous salvation.

Then Abraham put forth his hand, and took the knife to slay
his son. But the angel of the Lord called to him from heaven,
and said, "Abraham, Abraham!" And he said, "Here am I."
He said, "Do not lay your hand on the lad or do anything to
him; for now I know that you fear God, seeing you have not
withheld your son, your only son, from me." (Genesis 22.10–12)

In the painting of 1635 in Leningrad (preparatory
drawing, British Museum, see cat. no. 55, figure 18),
Rembrandt had depicted this climactic moment with great
Baroque animation and theatricality. In *Abraham and
Isaac* of 1645 (cat. no. 55), as we have seen, he chose rather
to examine a previous moment in the narrative, one that
permitted him to explore the elemental spiritual conflicts
of Abraham's conscience. *Abraham's Sacrifice* of 1655
marks a return to the portrayal of the dramatic moment
of sacrifice halted by the intercession of an angel. But
the exciting diagonal composition of the 1635 version, its
brutal realism and theatrical devices—including the knife
ripped from Abraham's hand and suspended in mid-air—
are replaced by a poignant focus on the emotions of the
patriarch and his son.

Details from the Biblical description are included (the
two servants and the ass left below and, barely visible in the
shadow behind the angel and unseen by Abraham, the
ram provided by the Lord), but there are also noteworthy
additions (the angel physically present, the young Isaac
poignantly held by his father rather than bound to an
altar, and the terrible basin set before the figures and
intended to receive the blood of Isaac). The descending
angel is still in motion, his wings open and his hair agitated
by the wind. Incisively Rembrandt conveys the innocent
submission of Isaac, whose head is supported against his
father, the shock of the suffering and only partially com-
prehending patriarch, the angel's tender, embracing gesture
of grace halting the deed, and the beams of heavenly
light that convey Divine benediction. Breaking through
the turbulent, dark atmosphere, so richly defined in
drypoint, that powerful light arrests and eternalizes this
terrible yet redemptive moment.

64 Abraham Entertaining the Angels

Date of execution: 1656

Definitive catalogues: H. 286; B., Holl. 29, state I/I

Process: etching and drypoint

Data on plate: lower left corner in shadow: Rembrandt f.1656

Data on print: on verso, top center: HHH (pencil); upper right
  corner: 2– (black ink); lower center: No 29_ (pencil); lower
  left: B.29 (pencil); below preceding: J.R.P. (?) (pencil);
  lower left corner: gEJ/EH (pencil); bottom center: B.29
  (pencil)

Dimensions: 159 mm x 131 mm (6¼″ x 5³⁄₁₆″) platemark
            166 mm x 138 mm (6½″ x 5⁷⁄₁₆″) sheet

Watermarks: –

Collections: on verso, lower left corner: Lugt 1070 (brown ink),
  "F. Gawet 1802. 16_" [F. Gawet, Vienna, 1762/65–1847];
  lower right corner: Lugt 2770b [Cortland F. Bishop, New York
  and Lenox, 1870–1935]; also, according to invoice from
  L. Papaharis: J. V. Novak, Prague, 1842–1918; A. E. McVitty
  (purchased at his sale, Parke Bernet, May 1949. lot 349);
  Read Mullan, Phoenix, Arizona; (L. Papaharis, March 11,
  1985)

Figure 24. Rembrandt, *Four Orientals Seated Beneath a Tree*,
pen and brown ink and wash, on Japanese paper, London,
British Museum

In the 1656 inventory of Rembrandt's possessions, item
203 is an album of "curieuse minijateur teeckeninge,"
Indo-Persian miniatures that he had acquired in about
1650. Rembrandt drew twenty studies from these Moghul
works, including a drawing on Japanese paper in the
British Museum (Benesch 1187, c. 1654–56, figure 24).
That drawing, a study of four dervishes beneath a tree,
based on a surviving miniature in the collection at
Schönbrunn Palace, Vienna, served the artist as the source
for this print, whose subject is found in Genesis 18.1–15.
Of the fifteen Old Testament subjects etched by Rembrandt, five concern Abraham. (This is the last print of a
Biblical scene created by the artist.) In an extraordinary
juxtaposition of sources, reflecting the breadth of the
artist's aesthetic interests, the youth with the bow (Ishmael?)
derives from one of the putti in the engraving by Marcantonio Raimondi after Raphael's *Galatea* (Bartsch 350).

Three men having suddenly appeared to Abraham
during the midday, he invites them to share his hospitality
and is depicted serving them milk and cakes prepared by
Sarah. The three angels are shown informing the patriarch
of the promised pregnancy of the aged Sarah, who, as
described in the Bible, upon hearing the prophecy laughs
to herself. The three angels are sharply differentiated.
The eldest (by my interpretation), who addresses Abraham
with the joyous tidings, has no wings, which has led to
the speculation, first advanced by Gersaint and followed
by Bartsch and White, that only two angels are shown:
that Abraham is entertaining the visitors on either side of
him and a servant is attending at right. There are other
inconsistencies: Sarah is set behind a cottage door rather
than a tent; Abraham does not stand by his visitors under
one of the oaks of Mamre; and the meal itself does not
take place beneath a tree (despite both the Biblical

description and the presence of a tree in the Moghul
drawing).

The Bible states that Abraham himself set the refresh-
ments before the angels, but also that Sarah was listening
at the door behind him. In a 1646 painted version of the
theme and two attributed preparatory drawings for it
(school productions? Benesch 576 and 577), the three
angels are seated together at the table and Abraham is
seated opposite them holding a drinking vessel. Sarah is
clearly visible behind him. Whatever the specifics of the
present depiction of this joyful, lighthearted story, it
makes an effective etching, and touches of drypoint
throughout the print enliven the scene.

Landscape

65 View of Amsterdam from the North West

Date of execution: c. 1640

Definitive catalogues: H. 176; B., Holl. 210, state I/I

Process: etching

Data on plate: –

Data on print: on verso, lower right: 17.—2 (brown ink); lower right corner: v (pencil)

Dimensions: 112 mm (125 mm) x 153 mm (4⅜″ [4¹⁵⁄₁₆″] x 6″) the upper platemark only lightly impressed and with a new platemark traced with a stylus 13 mm. higher, thus falsely indicating a new first state
127 mm x 156 mm (5″ x 6⅜″) sheet

Watermarks: –

Collections: on verso, lower right corner: R.E. (gray ink); (Sotheby Parke Bernet, New York, May 4, 1983, lot 58)

Rembrandt printed 27 landscapes, all executed between 1640 and 1653. They are tied to actual observations of the Dutch countryside and always are personalized by the inclusion of human activities and constructions. Furthermore Rembrandt's perspective vision approaches the natural one of a landscape seen by a standing person, neither the raised perspective of the early seventeenth-century mannerists nor the more naturalistic but still somewhat raised and sweeping perspective view of such tonal painters of the next generation as Salomon van Ruysdael and Jan van Goyen.

This view of Amsterdam, quite exact but reversed, as if the artist had drawn on the etching plate from life, is among his first landscape etchings. The view is taken from Bickers Island, then known as Kadijk, only a fifteen-minute walk from his home. From left to right the outstanding landmarks are the distant tower of Herrings Packers, the Oude Kerk, the tower of Montelbaans, the warehouses of the East and West India Company, the windmill of Rijzenhoofd, and the Zuiderkerk. Not shown are the West India Company warehouse (1642) and the Waleneiland (1644), providing a *terminus ante quem*. The middle ground is virtually lost in this natural viewpoint as the water channels guide the eye to the jagged, picturesque skyline of the port city. Through variations in the density of his etching within a limited tonal range and the nervous flow of the etching needle by which forms seem to shimmer, the artist suggests the actual view observed through a palpable atmosphere.

66 The Windmill

Date of execution: 1641

Definitive catalogues: H. 179; B., Holl. 233, state I/I

Process: etching

Data on plate: lower right corner: Rembrandt f 1641

Data on print: on verso, upper right corner: 68_(?) (pencil); lower right center: c. 34063 (pencil); lower left corner: 52 (pencil); below preceding: /2140 (pencil); lower right corner: 82A (pencil)

Dimensions: 145 mm x 204 mm (5¾" x 8¹⁄₁₆") trimmed to platemark with thread lines

Watermarks: partial coat of arms with fleur-de-lys (see Heawood 625)

Collections: on verso, lower left corner: Lugt 58 [Earl of Aylesford, London, 1786–1859]; (W. H. Schab, August 23, 1982)

In this depiction, one might say portrait, of a windmill, Rembrandt adopts a dramatic and extraordinarily imposing perspective on his subject, thrusting it as close as possible into the foreground and overwhelming its setting by its dominant form. The artist's febrile work with the etching needle defines the mill's surfaces and textures, its tiles, bricks, cracks, moss, and clinging vegetation, as though examining an aged face; yet the details themselves are subordinated in the soft, humid light to the mill's monumental profile. Gradually details of human daily activity emerge: the man with a sack of grain approaching the ladder to enter the windmill; the woman washing her clothes; the figures coming over the horizon.

Clearly the constantly shifting network of parallel strokes animates the composition, but the enveloping gray atmosphere also plays a prominent role in providing a uniform tone to the piece. As in other works of the time (e.g. cat. nos. 18 and 20), Rembrandt has achieved an extraordinary, gray wash-like surface tone by applying a sulfur tint, causing cracks in the varnish/resin visible as grain and craquelure. Although Christopher White contends that the effect was caused accidentally by uneven burnishing of the copper plate, rather than deliberately by adding a sulfur tint, as Ackley has noted the controlled range of tone and small corrosive dotting of the plate indicate an intentional process, achieving in this print sublime effects of an overcast sky with denser cloud layers.

The windmill, situated near one of the rampart bastions of Amsterdam at Lauriergracht, was called "de Passeerder." It was not, as sometimes contended in the older literature (including Gersaint), the mill owned by Rembrandt's family near the ramparts of Leyden. A proof of this print in the collection of the Rembrandt-Huis in Amsterdam carries an old inscription "den wyntmolen van den pester van Ossen-bruggen," identified by J. G. van Gelder (*Oud Holland*, 1938, pp. 8–9; and 1939, p. 87) as the mill of Rembrandt's maternal grandfather near Leyden; however, a drawing formerly at Bremen (Benesch 810), viewing the present mill from a different angle and at a greater distance, clearly identifies the site near Amsterdam.

The exhibited brilliant impression is a very early and delicately inked one with notably rich inking of the arms of the windmill and the shadows beneath the gallery. The gentle, evocative atmospheric effects achieved by Rembrandt through the use and partial burnishing out of the sulfur tints make this print one of the finest and most beautiful of all known impressions of *The Windmill*.

67 The Three Trees

Date of execution: 1643

Definitive catalogues: H. 205; B., Holl. 212, state I/I

Process: etching, drypoint, and burin

Data on plate: lower left corner: Rembrandt f 1643

Data on print: on verso, lower left corner: y (pencil); JSO.LOV
(pencil); x-1336 (pencil); bottom center: 204 (pencil)

Dimensions: 213 mm x 282 mm (8⅜″ x 11¼₆″) platemark
221 mm x 288 mm (8¹¹⁄₁₆″ x 11⁵⁄₁₆″) sheet

Watermarks: partial with letters WK (according to Susan Pinsky
at Sotheby's, New York, a lily-in-crowned-shield watermark;
see *Rembrandt: Experimental Etcher* [Boston: Museum of
Fine Arts; New York: Pierpont Morgan Library, 1969], p. 181,
watermark 1, figure 1, p. 182, c. 1646). Watermark also
appears similar to Heawood 1666.

Collections: Lugt 1692 (black ink) [F. Locker Lampson, Sussex,
1821–1895] (in sale Christie's, London, December 20, 1918,
among lots 136–143, for £1123/10s, mentioned in Lugt);
(Sotheby Parke Bernet, New York, February 16, 1979, lot 694);
(Sotheby's, New York, private sale, July 3, 1986)

The Three Trees is the most famous of Rembrandt's
landscapes, exhibited here in a truly magnificent, dark,
and sensitively inked impression. It is also his most dramatic
and technically stunning landscape etching, with a Baroque
romanticism generally associated with his works of the
1630s. It is to Gersaint that we owe the title "The Three
Trees." Indeed, their dark, massed profile against the
bright, open sky is the focal motif of the composition, in
which we find not only a comprehensive range of atmospheric effects but also an encyclopedic repertoire of
human activities.

Insofar as the print has a subject, it would seem to be
the very cycle of nature and human action. As the swiftly
moving storm darkens the left side of the composition and
the light descends through the breaking clouds, we are
reminded of the rapidly changing weather common in the
flat landscape of the Netherlands. The directionality of
the strokes and the unhurried activities of the human
participants would seem to indicate that the storm is
departing rather than arriving, yet the psychological
impression is to the contrary. The site is unspecific, but
the city so delicately etched in the background, as if
vibrating before our eyes in the dense, humid air, has
been identified as Amsterdam. The light falling on the
middle-ground valley at left is critical in opening up the
space and providing the sense of sweeping depth beneath
the active sky with its looming storm.

Although the dynamic sky and the stunning light-to-dark
contrasts it precipitates may be the protagonists of this
natural drama, the print is also, in a sense, a microcosm,
one whose details gradually emerge from the landscape
and its shadows. Most obvious are the fisherman and his
wife watching their rod and dangling bait. Behind them
a herdsman guards his cattle, and less defined groups are
visible marching in the sunlit valley behind him. On the
hillock a carriage full of people approaches a draftsman,
isolated in light, who is sketching the landscape. There
are also more shadowed activities in the foreground
shrubbery, notably the lovers in the bower. Animal life
abounds: the grazing cattle, a horse barely visible in the
right foreground, a migrating flock of birds and a single
bird soaring to the left of the three trees.

The landscape is also architecturally varied. In the
distance is the city of Amsterdam, in the middle ground
a village and one of several windmills are visible, and on
the right, almost obscured by the three trees, is a cottage.
The print relies on a masterly combination of etching,
drypoint, and burin to achieve its varied light effects. As
Christopher White has noted, this is the first landscape
in which Rembrandt used drypoint. The technique is
visible in the underdrawing of shadows, the enframing
clouds above Amsterdam at the top of the plate, and the
extraordinary, long parallel streaks of sunrays and shadow
in the diagonally descending rain showers at left, an
unforgettable effect repeated a decade later in *The Three
Crosses* (B., Holl. 78). Rembrandt also apparently immersed
the foreground of the plate in the acid bath longer than
the rest of the print to achieve the deep black shadows.

The rich variations in inking in this superb impression
powerfully convey the threatening, looming movement
and verticality of the distant thunderclouds over the city,
the streaks of violent rainfall, and the profile of the three
trees silhouetted so majestically in the raking light. As
Ackley has suggested, the artist also appears to have
experimented again with sulfur-tinting the plate (see *The
Windmill*, cat. no. 66) to gain the granular tones of the
rapidly moving shadows over the field. In this early
impression he seems to have combined this technique,
partially burnished out, with plate tone in the sky.

68 The Shepherd and His Family

Date of execution: 1644
Definitive catalogues: H. 206; B., Holl. 220, state I/I
Process: etching
Data on plate: upper left corner: Rembrandt f. 1644
Data on print: –
Dimensions: 95 mm x 67 mm (3¾″ x 2⅝″) platemark
            110 mm x 83 mm (4⅜″ x 3¼″) sheet
Watermarks: –
Collections: (Sotheby's, London, November 28, 1979, lot 951);
    (Sotheby Parke Bernet, New York, May 4, 1983, lot 59)

The Shepherd and His Family, one of only three small
plates that constitute Rembrandt's graphic production
in 1644, is a synthesis of genre scene and landscape. The
foreground figures and their flock do not dominate their
setting, but are conceived as inextricable elements within
a greater experiential whole. In this idyllic pastoral, as in
works of the Venetian Renaissance—a school that interested
Rembrandt in the 1640s and 1650s (see cat. nos. 19 and
56, and *St. Jerome Reading in an Italian Landscape* [B.,
Holl. 104])—nature not only complements but augments
the sensibility and mood of the work.

Unusually for Rembrandt, the figures hardly relate to
each other in this composition, perhaps precisely because
they are perceived within this broader, Giorgionesque
context. Indeed, one is reminded of drawings and prints of
landscapes with figures by both Giulio and Domenico
Campagnola and drawings by the young Titian. (A contemporary example of this type of landscape drawing by
Rembrandt, in this case a copy of a drawing by the young
Titian in the collection of the Fondation Custodia, Paris,
was proposed and published by Konrad Oberhuber, *Disegni
di Tiziano e della sua cerchia*, Venice, 1976, figure 7.) In
Rembrandt's 1656 inventory, item 216 is "Een dito seer
groot, met meest alle de wercken van Titian" (one ditto
[book] very large with almost all the work of Titian).

69 The Omval

Date of execution: 1645

Definitive catalogues: H. 210; B., Holl. 209, state II/II

Process: etching and drypoint

Data on plate: lower right corner: Rembrant 1645

Data on print: on verso, lower left center: B.209 (pencil); lower right: 41 in (pencil); U.U. (pencil); bottom left: 209 (pencil); below preceding: 6267 (pencil); bottom right: 209 (pencil)

Dimensions: 186 mm x 226 mm (7⁵⁄₁₆″ x 8¹⁵⁄₁₆″) platemark
189 mm x 230 mm (7⁷⁄₁₆″ x 9¹⁄₁₆″) sheet

Watermarks: in center, initials PR and lily in straight-sided shield

Collections: on verso, lower left center: Lugt 1672 [Graf von Lepell, Germany, 1755–1826]; lower right center: Lugt 1606 [Berlin Print Room] and above it Lugt 2398 [Berlin Print Room duplicate]; (Sotheby's, London, May 15, 1986, lot 78)

The Omval is the bend of the Amstel River between Amsterdam and Ouderkerk, an area that in the seventeenth century encompassed a few buildings and a windmill. Rembrandt made several drawings of the Omval, one of which (Benesch 1347) represents the same location seen in reverse but without the aged willow trunk. The same trunk appears to have served as the inspiration for *St. Jerome Beside a Pollard Willow* of 1648 (cat. no. 56). Rembrandt has drawn the far bank of the Amstel closer in the etching, however, and made it seem more accessible by breaking down the planar divisions of the composition through the graduated interstices on the right of the small tree trunk, the figure standing on the tow path, and the holiday boat on the river. Other subtle connecting orthogonals between the broad riverbanks are the lightly etched sailboats and wharf. At the same time, the massive, ancient, gnarled willow and the wild vegetation with hidden lovers in the foreground provide a foil to the suburban life on the opposite bank and along the river. The opposition, or juxtaposition, of untamed and shaded nature with the brightly lit civilized pastimes on the Omval was certainly the artist's intent; however, he does not clearly present us with an allegory. If there are intimations of a deeper meaning, it remains for the viewer to interpret them.

Drypoint is used more integrally in this print than in *The Three Trees* (cat. no. 67), accentuating the willow and deepening the shadows. By applying the drypoint over a ground already etched in cross-hatching, Rembrandt does not have to vary the exposure of portions of the copper plate to the acid bath. Furthermore, the drypoint, which plays an active role in defining the rushes, trees, and willow trunk in the foreground and dramatically setting them in rich tonal distinction from the far bank, not only contributes to the contrast in light, but also establishes perceptual space within the image. Within the verdant obscurity to the left of the tree, a pair of young lovers are partially hidden, the male placing a crown of flowers on the forehead of his beloved.

70 Cottages and Farm Buildings with a Man Sketching

Date of execution: c. 1645

Definitive catalogues: H. 213; B., Holl. 219, state I/I

Process: etching

Data on plate: –

Data on print: on verso, lower left center: Rembrandt B219
enige staat (pencil); below "staat": B219 (pencil); lower right:
c.38117 (pencil); lower right corner: -1 (red pencil); Sp.48
(red pencil); W216 (pencil); lower left corner ▲ =52 (pencil)

Dimensions: 131 mm x 209 mm (5⅛" x 8¼") platemark
138 mm x 214 mm (5⁷⁄₁₆" x 8⁷⁄₁₆") sheet

Watermarks: –

Collections: (The Laurentuis, Netherlands, November 25, 1985)

Two drawings by Rembrandt can be associated specifically with the thatched cottage depicted in this print
(Benesch 473, c. 1639; Benesch 816, c. 1645); both are in
reverse to the print. The farmstead in the latter drawing is
especially similar to the one in the etching.

In the right foreground a draftsman (Rembrandt
himself?), reminiscent of the figure in *The Three Trees*
(cat. no. 67), is in the process of sketching the scene before
him. The print, executed entirely in etching, shaded with
simple, open cross-hatching, and delicately printed, has
the vividness, lightness, and informality of a rapid sketch,
full of picturesque details, drawn outdoors. The exhibited
print is a particularly cleanly inked, crisp impression in
which the sensation of bright sunlight is effectively
suggested in the open, uninked fields by the paper itself.

71 Cottage with a White Paling

Date of execution: 1648
Definitive catalogues: H. 203; B., Holl. 232, state III/III
Process: etching and drypoint
Data on plate: bottom left center: Rembrandt f, 1648
Data on print: on verso, lower left: an gell___ (pencil); below
    preceding: No. 24 (black chalk); lower right: u (pencil)
Dimensions: 130 mm x 159 mm (5⅛″ x 6¼″) platemark
            132 mm x 161 mm (5³⁄₁₆″ x 6⁵⁄₁₆″) sheet
Watermarks: –
Collections: on verso, lower extreme left: Lugt 791 [Dr. W. A.
    Ackermann, Lubeck and Dresden, 1793–1865]; lower left
    center: Lugt 176 [H. Danby Seymour, London and Trent,
    1820–1877]; (Kornfeld und Klipstein, Bern, auction 179,
    June 26, 1981, lot 167)

The site is near Diemen on the Sint Anthonius Dike. An
unusually finished and close preparatory study for the
etching, in reverse (Benesch C.41; Benesch considers the
drawing a faithful copy), survives in a private American
collection. According to White, the noteworthy similarity
of the study to the print may indicate that the final design
was worked up in the studio. Among minor changes, the
man with his back to the viewer seated and looking out
on the water is set farther back in the print, and the man
and cow on the horizon to the right are added, as are the
ducks in the foreground. The wooden planks before the
cottage are somewhat different in the print; also the tree
behind the paling is reduced in scale, and both trees are
flattened at top, creating a more unified and monolithic
block of cottage, paling, and trees. This increased emphasis
on horizontals, by which the central haystack behind the
cottage also gains more prominence, opens up the landscape so that the eye can travel back to the horizon line.
The composition is less dramatic and humbler than *The
Windmill* (cat. no. 66). The change between the first and
second states (the third was constituted by the addition
of the date), the shading of the dike to the left of the
cottage, enhances the spatial recession of the composition.

In this fine, well-inked impression of the third state,
the artist's ability to articulate the density of the tree
branches while still conveying their lightness through
varying patterns of nervous short strokes is wonderfully
apparent. Noteworthy also is the way the still, mirror-like
surface and density of the water are expressed by the
contrast between the long, wide strokes of the actual
objects and the short, febrile, shimmering lines of their
reflections.

The attention the artist has paid to the inking of this
specific impression is apparent in such details as the black
areas beneath the thatched roof and along the bank.
There is much burr in the foreground bank, the chimney,
the haystack, the tree on the right, and the shadow of the
wagon at right, establishing both space and the sensation
of the dappling flow of natural light. Traces of plate tone
are visible alongside the man at left. The warm, golden-
toned paper on which the etching is printed also
contributes significantly to its appeal.

72 Canal with a Large Boat and Bridge (Het Schuytje op de Voorgrondt)

Date of execution: 1650

Definitive catalogues: H. 239; B., Holl. 236, state II/II

Process: etching and drypoint

Data on plate: bottom left center: Rembrandt f.1650 (d and 6 reversed)

Data on print: on verso, upper left: 236 (black ink); upper center: 227 (pencil)

Dimensions: 83 mm x 109 mm (3⅝″ x 4⅝″) platemark
84 mm x 110 mm (3⅝″ x 4⅝″) sheet trimmed just outside of platemark with rounded corners at top

Watermarks: fragment of a watermark with circles (bottom of foolscap?) in upper corner

Collections: on recto, bottom center: Lugt 2200 (dry) [A. P. F. Robert-Dumesnil, Paris, 1778–1864] (probably in sale cited in Lugt entry: Phillips, London, April 12, 1836); on verso, lower left corner: Lugt 719a [Viscount Downe, Wykeham Abbey, Scarborough, b. 1903]; (Sotheby's, London, July 9, 1985, lot 412)

This intimate landscape, for all its informality, is actually carefully composed in a series of parallel receding planes of varying light. In the right foreground drypoint is particularly rich in this beautifully inked early impression of the second state. Enriching the shadows of the tree and the grasses of the far bank, it forcefully establishes the foreground plane and the middle ground. The wooden bridge and quay connect those planes. The cliffs at the extreme left are counterposed with the tree in the right foreground; drawn sketchily, they recede into the distance. The loosely etched, dense woods enclose the town, and the shading of the village and the central church tower serves both to distinguish the solid architecture from the enveloping shrubbery and to draw the viewer back into the distant space. The sensitive inking and golden, ivory tone of the paper itself help to create the impression of forms seen through a palpable atmosphere.

73 Landscape with a Cow

Date of execution: c. 1650
Definitive catalogues: H. 240; B., Holl. 237, state II/II
Process: etching and drypoint
Data on plate: –
Data on print: on verso, center: Daulby 228 (pencil); Wilson
     234 (pencil); Bar. 237 (pencil); lower left: 7774 (pencil); cc
     (pencil); 241 (pencil); lower center: c.18145 (pencil); bottom
     center: B.227 (WZ) (pencil); J.4351 (pencil)
Dimensions: 103 mm x 130 mm (4$\frac{1}{16}$″ x 5$\frac{1}{8}$″) platemark
             107 mm x 131 mm (4$\frac{3}{16}$″ x 5$\frac{3}{16}$″) sheet trimmed
                to platemark at top
Watermarks: partial LR top center
Collections: on recto, bottom left: Lugt 2090 [P. H. Lankrink,
     London, 1628–1692]; lower left corner: Lugt 892 [Dr. E. Peart,
     London and Butterwick, 1756–1824]; (Christie's, London,
     April 12, 1822, lot 69, to Smith); on verso, lower left: Lugt
     1250 [T. C. D. Hebich, Hamburg, 1818–1891]; (Christie's,
     London, June 17, 1981, lot 106a)

   Much burr is visible, especially along the canal bank,
in yet another beautifully inked impression on golden-tan
paper, pulled early in the second state. Like the preceding
print (cat. no. 72) of the same year, the composition
juxtaposes an imaginary mountain with a landscape quite
common to Holland and familiar in the work of Rembrandt. The thatch cottage may be the same as the one in
a contemporary drawing seen from another angle (Benesch
1228). It is in any case very similar, and both the cottage
and the trees are rendered in the same drawing style. The
site has been identified as along the Sint Anthonius Dike
near Diemen. The etching is light and delicate, and the
foreground plane is established in drypoint. Note how
the cliff behind the cottage shimmeringly dissolves into the
distance as a result of the delicate etching and inking of
this impression.

74 Landscape with a Milkman ('Het Melkboertje')

Date of execution: c. 1650

Definitive catalogues: H. 242; B., Holl. 213, state II/II

Process: etching and drypoint

Data on plate: –

Data on print: on verso, lower right base: R4157 (pencil); C11341 (pencil); C9986 (pencil)

Dimensions: 65 mm x 175 mm (2 9/16″ x 6 15/16″) platemark
67 mm x 178 mm (2 5/8″ x 7″) sheet

Watermarks: –

Collections: on verso, lower center: Lugt 1790 (brown ink), "P. mariette 1672" [Pierre Mariette II, Paris, 1634–1716]; (Sotheby's, New York, November 20, 1986, lot 54)

Described by Christopher White as one of the quintessential representations of the landscape near Amsterdam, the view is from Diemedyk toward the Zuyder Zee, proceeding along the dike. Below and to the left is a farmhouse, with a second one visible beyond it; to the right, in the distance, is a view of the Ij River with the contours of its busy cargoes dissolving in the sunlight. The compressed, stolid domestic scene occupying the foreground and the left is balanced harmoniously against the calm, open waterway on the right. As in cat. no. 78 of 1652, etching and drypoint are totally integrated to create a continuous, softly modulating tonal range. In the second state, exhibited here, the artist has burnished the plate slightly to further soften the transitions from the darker black of the milkman and the grasses to the shadows by the farmhouse and trees to the lightly etched horizon and ships. He also has added the lightly etched horizon at left to balance the one at right.

Two related drawings of the farmhouses survive, Benesch 836 (c. 1648–50) and Benesch 1227 (c. 1650), the latter serving as a preparatory study for the print; as usual, the drawings are in reverse to the composition of the print. In both drawings the artist has focused from a lower angle entirely on the farmstead and path. Only in the final print did he expand the scope of the composition. The farm in the center middle ground appears to be the same as that featured in cat. no. 74, seen from another angle. Although the traditional title of the print is "Het Melkboertje," in 1963 Boon suggested that the milkman accompanied by his dog might actually be a fisherman returning with his catch.

This impression is another fine, richly inked and toned print, with much burr, especially in the left foreground and in the partially burnished tall grasses at right. It is printed on ivory-toned paper.

75 Landscape with an Obelisk

Date of execution: c. 1650

Definitive catalogues: H. 243; B., Holl. 227, state II/II

Process: etching, drypoint, and burin

Data on plate: –

Data on print: on verso, lower center: B 227 II (pencil); lower
    left: c/_/_ mf (pencil); lower right: c.224455 (pencil); bottom
    left: 212006,1 (black ink)

Dimensions: 84 mm x 162 mm (3⁵⁄₁₆″ x 6⅜″) platemark
            87 mm x 165 mm (3⁷⁄₁₆″ x 6½″) sheet

Watermarks: partial watermark top center: coat of arms (?)
    with letters IR

Collections: on verso, upper right: Lugt 1420 (brown ink) [John
    Barnard, London, d. 1784]; lower right and left: Lugt 2213a
    [R. Gutekunst, Bern, b. 1870]; (Lugt 719a, Viscount Downe,
    Wykeham Abbey, Scarborough, b. 1903, according to invoice,
    no stamp); (Kennedy Galleries, September 16, 1980)

The monument in the left foreground of the *Landscape
with an Obelisk* is actually the boundary marker at
Halfweg, the limit of the jurisdiction of Amsterdam,
halfway between that city and Haarlem. Within the outer
contours of the obelisk one can still make out the complete
originally drawn monument block, with its peak meeting
the top of the plate, a feature replaced by the enlarged
and truncated final form. The view itself defines the close
cottages and chimneys and the unlimited fields at right.
Thus the composition is organized in a simple diagonal,
progressing step by step from left to right.

As in cat. no. 74, Rembrandt burnished out some of the
heavier drypoint burr in the second state, especially in
the thatched roof and foreground shrubbery and grasses.
He replaced it with burin and added areas of shadow,
notably at the base of the obelisk and in the roofs of
the distant cottages, to achieve a greater uniformity of
tone. By carefully controlling the tonal balance to make
the cottage and tree at center both the strongly lit and
darkly inked focus of the landscape, Rembrandt is able to
include the monumental obelisk at left without overwhelming the rest of the composition.

The second state is here presented in yet another fine
impression, with a warm film of plate tone and rich
drypoint burr, printed on golden-tan paper.

76 Landscape with Three Gabled Cottages Beside a Road

Date of execution: 1650

Definitive catalogues: H. 246; B., Holl. 217, state III/III

Process: etching and drypoint

Data on plate: lower left corner: Rembrandt f 1650

Data on print: on verso, lower center: th/ B.P.318-4et (pencil); B.217-3et (pencil); below preceding: Paysage au trois chaumières (pencil); lower left corner: G 94 (pencil); below preceding: s vz/_ (pencil); fr 220/vgbi (pencil); bottom center: c.4 (pencil); lower right corner: c. 31670 (pencil)

Dimensions: 161 mm x 204 mm (6⅜″ x 8 1/16″) platemark
164 mm x 209 mm (6 7/16″ x 8 3/16″) sheet

Watermarks: Arms of Amsterdam (Churchill 5)

Collections: on verso, lower left center: Lugt 1962 [Neville D. Goldsmid, The Hague, 1814–1875]; lower left corner: Lugt 1206 [Georg Rath, Budapest, 1828–1904] (print cited by Lugt in Rath sale, A. Posonyi, Vienna, January 11–, 1869); (Christie's, London, June 24, 1986, lot 302)

A drawing of three cottages executed c. 1640 (Benesch 795, facing the same direction as the print) is preserved at the Nationalmuseum in Stockholm and seems to have served as the source for this print. Rembrandt altered the profiles of the buildings and set them farther back into the center middle ground, also adding a single, tall tree in the right foreground and a path guiding the eye diagonally across the sheet into the distance. He seems to have enjoyed working with this compositional arrangement at this time. The same general format is also employed in cat. no. 75 of the same year and the *Clump of Trees with a Vista* (B., Holl. 222) of 1652.

Here drypoint is used more dramatically than in cat. nos. 73–75 and 78 to articulate rich shadows and to highlight the dense foliage over the cottages, captured in sunlight and swaying in the breeze. Indeed, the artist seems actively to be seeking these richer, more painterly effects in the evolution of the print. The second and third states are each distinguished by the addition of shadow. The present impression constitutes the third state in a very fine impression, distinguished by particularly sensitive wiping effects about the trees and rushes on the right and rich drypoint burr throughout.

77 The Goldweigher's Field

Date of execution: 1651

Definitive catalogues: H. 249; B., Holl. 234, state I/I

Process: etching and drypoint

Data on plate: lower left corner: Rembrandt 1651

Data on print: on verso, lower left: Bartsch 234 (pencil)

Dimensions: 121 mm x 317 mm (4¾" x 12½") trimmed to edge or just within platemark

Watermarks: fragment of a crown surmounting a fleur-de-lys, similar to crown in Heawood 2842, but not identical

Collections: on verso, upper left corner: indecipherable stamp; (Christie's, New York, May 10, 1982, lot 86)

The traditional name for this print derives from the 1751 catalogue raisonné (no. 226) of Gersaint, who confused this landscape with another (*Landscape with Trees, Farm Buildings, and a Tower*, B., Holl. 223) mentioned in Valerius Röver's collection inventory (1731 [see commentary on Röver, cat. no. 10]). The goldweigher, the Receiver General Jan Uytenbogaert, whose property is depicted in the other etching, was also the subject of a portrait print by Rembrandt (B., Holl. 281). The land in the foreground of the present composition, including the estate called Saxenburg and the summer pavilion with swans at left, actually belonged to the merchant Christoffel Thijs, who had sold Rembrandt his mansion house on Breestraat in 1639 and to whom Rembrandt was still in arrears. The view is from the dune called "het Kopje," and the city of Haarlem with the spire of the Grootekerk is visible at left. In the right middle ground is the church tower of Bloemendaal.

A contemporary study of the site from a slightly different angle (Benesch 1259) was used for the etching. The drawing was made during one of Rembrandt's visits to his creditor and may well have been one of several adapted to the more expansive view in the final print. A painting of the landscape that includes a portrait of Thijs hunting (Los Angeles, private collection) is attributed by some scholars to the artist. As usual, the print is in reverse to the drawing and the painting. As has often been noted, this type of extended horizontal panorama appeared earlier in Dutch art in prints by Pieter Bast, Jan van de Velde, Hercules Seghers, Johannes Ruisscher, and others.

Again Rembrandt has created the semblance of a totally naturalistic and unmanipulated view in a carefully organized composition, in this case captured from an unusually low perspective for such views, as though seen by someone standing on the dune. The separate planes of the composition are subtly integrated through diagonal divisions in the fields, and the horizontals of the property divisions and the cope of woods with the Bloemendaalkerk retard the perceptual movement to the horizon. The drypoint is used to accent and enliven the composition, creating dark shadows in the brightly lit plain. Its touches throughout convey the sensation of forms seen in midday sun, a light that dissolves details as it streams over forms.

Although only one state of the print exists, individual impressions vary widely in clarity and intensity of burr. In the earliest impressions intense and somewhat blurry dark areas of shadow in the left foreground and the middle ground to the left of the Bloemendaalkerk tend to detract from the carefully composed recession to the horizon. Slightly later impressions, like the present one, still early and executed before the wearing down of the plate, seem to have been modified by gentle, selective burnishing to create a proper tonal balance. Such impressions therefore embody the artist's fully realized intentions.

78 Landscape with a Hay Barn and a Flock of Sheep

Date of execution: 1652

Definitive catalogues: H. 241; B., Holl. 224, state II/II

Process: etching and drypoint

Data on plate: lower left base: Rembrandt f 1652 (the d is reversed)

Data on print: on verso, partially obscured, upper center: 8/1 (brown ink); lower right base: K4156 (pencil); c 11342 (pencil); c.9985 (pencil)

Dimensions: 82 mm x 173 mm (3¼″ x 6¹³⁄₁₆″) platemark
84 mm x 174 mm (3⁵⁄₁₆″ x 6⅞″) sheet trimmed to just outside platemark

Watermarks: –

Collections: (Sotheby's, New York, November 20, 1986, lot 56)

This print is one of a group of late landscapes (e.g. cat. nos. 73, 74, 75) in which the artist portrays intimate landscapes in a carefully orchestrated middle range of tones. These late, small, utterly simple pastoral themes have reminded Jakob Rosenberg of similar subjects in the drawings of Bruegel and his circle, but they possess firmer structure and a greater conviction of perceived reality. The small, concentrated composition, focusing on a single farmstead with only a brief sketch of a nearby cottage and the briefest pictorial suggestion of a distant town and the far horizon, was drawn with the etching needle. The same farm, from another angle, appears in cat. no. 74. Rembrandt then worked in drypoint on the plate. In other, earlier landscapes executed in mixed techniques (e.g. *The Three Trees*, cat. no. 67), each technique was used for its own readily identifiable contribution to the whole; here the processes are so subtly integrated that they are virtually indistinguishable. The resulting print is an image of great tonal precision and uniformity with soft, atmospheric modulations of shadow. In this fine impression with rich inking and much burr in the shadows, the enveloping tonal unity is enhanced by the warm tonality of the paper.

79 Landscape with Sportsman and Dog ('Het Jagertje')

Date of execution: c. 1653

Definitive catalogues: H. 265; B., Holl. 211, state II/II

Process: etching and drypoint (touches of gray wash added in the branches upper right)

Data on plate: –

Data on print: on verso, upper right: <u>6</u> (brown ink); base center: B 211 II (pencil); H 265 II (pencil); c 25891 (pencil)

Dimensions: 128 mm x 157 mm (5⅟₁₆″ x 6³⁄₁₆″) platemark 130 mm x 159 mm (5⅛″ x 6¼″) sheet

Watermarks: top center: fragment of fleur-de-lys in straight-sided shield

Collections: (Lugt 719a, Viscount Downe, Wykeham Abbey, Scarborough, b. 1903, his sale, Sotheby's, London, December 7, 1972, lot 164, no stamp); (Sotheby's, New York, November 20, 1986, lot 53)

A most appropriate concluding image to this catalogue, the classically balanced pastoral image of "het Jagertje" (the hunter) is the last landscape print Rembrandt created. In it he looks beyond the immediately accessible landscapes of his native Holland, a land he never left, and imagines, in the distance beyond the middle ground with its village and church, steep mountains. In one of the foothills are situated the romanticized ruins of a Roman amphitheater. As opposed to the infinitely extended, open horizon of *The Goldweigher's Field* (cat. no. 77), the landscape is enclosed. The composition is primarily etched. Drypoint is used to emphasize details of the primary motifs, determining the spatial rythm of the composition and isolating the human figure, by whose scale we measure the landscape. (Note the effective, underlining shadow cast by the hunter.) As White has noted, the hunter is larger than any figure previously portrayed by Rembrandt in a landscape print.

The print is personalized, made intimate by such charming subsidiary details as the ducks in the left foreground and the birds approaching and landing on the upper branches of the tree in the right foreground. The Italian, especially Venetian, influence often noted in this print is manifested not only in the picturesque ancient ruins and the exotic element of the rounded mountain range, but also in the classical balance of the composition.

Some acid corrosion and toning is visible by the base of the tree in the foreground. The artist worked hard to achieve tonal balance in the work, burnishing out over-assertive details of a cottage and a hay barn and softening the shading of the foothills at left, thus opening up the space and distilling the perception of broad, massive forms seemingly dissolving in atmosphere.

Biographical Chronology

1 6 0 6. July 15, birth in Leyden of Rembrandt Harmenszoon van Rijn, the eighth of nine children, to Harmen Gerritszoon van Rijn, a miller, and Neeltgen Willemsdochter van Zuybroek (various spellings: Neeltje van Snydtbroeck), the daughter of a baker.

1 6 2 0. May 20, registration of Rembrandt as a student at the University of Leyden, after seven years of instruction at the Latin School at Leyden. After several months he leaves to study under Jacob Swanenburgh (1571–1638), a late mannerist painter, who specialized in portraits, architectural scenes, and fantasies in the style of Bosch.

1 6 2 4. The young artist spends six months in Amsterdam, working in the studio of Pieter Lastman (1583–1633), a successful and influential painter of religious and mythological subjects. Lastman had studied in Italy, where he had been influenced by the works of Caravaggio and Elsheimer. Unlike Rembrandt's previous master, Lastman has a profound impact upon Rembrandt, both stylistically and in his choice of subject matter and mode of depiction. While in Amsterdam, Rembrandt acquaints himself with the work of Elsheimer, Hercules Seghers, and the Utrecht Caravaggists. The same year he returns to Leyden and sets up an independent studio.

1 6 2 5. His first dated painting: *The Stoning of Saint Stephen* (Lyon, Musée des Beaux-Arts).

1 6 2 6. Joins in partnership with the artist Jan Lievens (1607–1674), who had also studied in the studio of Lastman. The two artists work in close collaboration.

1 6 2 8. Rembrandt's first dated etchings (two small portraits of his mother, cf. cat. no. 1). Gerrit Dou (1613–1675) enters his studio as his first student.

1 6 3 0. April 27, the burial of Rembrandt's father. In this year Rembrandt is visited by Constantijn Huygens, who, in a Latin manuscript, lauds the youth, comparing his genius favorably with those of Protogenes, Apelles, and Parthesius, and, more pointedly, states that Rembrandt is superior to Lievens "in judgment and in the liveliness of emotion." Executes several etched portrait studies and self-portraits (cf. cat. nos. 2–4) and studies of beggars (e.g. cat. nos. 26–30).

1 6 3 1. Moves in the autumn to Amsterdam, where he installs himself on the Sint Anthoniesbreestraat in the house of Hendrick van Uylenburch, a dealer in paintings, a Mennonite and a prominent businessman in whose house people interested in the arts commonly met. The artist rapidly becomes the portraitist of fashion in this cosmopolitan city. *Jupiter and Antiope: Smaller Plate* (cat. no. 31).

1 6 3 2. Receives his first important commission, the group portrait *The Anatomy Lesson of Professor Tulp* (The Hague, Mauritshuis).

1 6 3 3. Executes the painting *The Descent from the Cross* (Alte Pinakothek, Munich), based on the earlier composition of Rubens. The picture is acquired by Frederick-Henry, Staathouder of Holland. About this time Rembrandt receives important commissions for three further scenes from the Passion from Frederick-Henry, executed over the next several years. *Jan Cornelis Sylvius, Preacher* (cat. no. 7).

1 6 3 4. On June 22 marries Saskia van Uylenburch, niece of his landlord and wealthy orphan of the influential burgomeister of Leeuwarden in Friesland. The Calvinist minister Jan Cornelis Sylvius is her guardian. *Joseph and Potiphar's Wife* (cat. no. 45).

1 6 3 5. Birth of his first child, a son named Rumbartus, in December. The child survives only two months. *The Great Jewish Bride* (cat. no. 10) and *The Quacksalver* (cat. no. 32).

1 6 3 6–3 8. Paints his first landscapes and the *Danae* (Leningrad, Hermitage, 1636). *Self Portrait with Saskia*, 1636 (cat. no. 12), *Abraham Casting Out Hagar and Ishmael*, 1637 (cat. no. 50), and *The Little Jewish Bride*, 1638 (cat. no. 16).

1 6 3 9. On April 9, attends an auction of Italian paintings, at which time he records Raphael's *Balthasar Castiglione* (Paris, Louvre). At the house of Alfonso Lopez, he also sees Titian's *Man with a Blue Sleeve* (London, National Gallery). These works have a great influence on him and are adapted to etched and painted self-portraits of the same and the following year, respectively. On May 1, he and Saskia move to a sumptuous mansion house at 4–6 Sint Anthoniesbreestraat, bought on credit on January 3, 1639, from the merchant Christoffel Thijs. The artist has already begun amassing the extensive art collection itemized in his 1656 bankruptcy inventory. *The Artist Drawing from the Model* (cat. no. 34).

1 6 4 0. In May his mother dies in Leyden.

1 6 4 1. September 22, the baptism of their infant son Titus (1641–1668), named after Saskia's aunt, at the Zuiderkerk. Their fourth child and the only one to survive infancy, he becomes a favorite subject for the artist and a devoted son during Rembrandt's financially troubled later years. In the same year, Jan Orlers publishes the first biography of the artist. *The Triumph of Mordecai* (cat. no. 51) and *The Windmill* (cat. no. 66).

1 6 4 2. Weakened by tuberculosis and her successive pregnancies, Saskia dies at the age of 30 on June 14. Rembrandt hires, as a nurse for his son, Geertge Dircx, a trumpeter's widow who ultimately becomes the artist's mistress. Difficulties arise in 1648 as Rembrandt's affections turn to the devoted Hendrickje Stoffels, a sergeant's daughter from Bredevoort, who had entered his household earlier in the decade. The outcome of this relationship is a breach-of-promise suit in 1649 that continues until 1650, when Geertge is imprisoned at Gouda as a result of misconduct and her mental state. Released in 1655, she dies shortly thereafter. Rembrandt paints the famous group portrait *The Night Watch* (*The Company of Captain Frans Banning Cocq*) (Amsterdam, Rijksmuseum) and the *David and Absalom* (Leningrad, Hermitage). *The Raising of Lazarus: Small Plate* (cat. no. 54) and *The Flute Player (L'Espiègle)* (cat. no. 36).

1 6 4 3–4 6. A period of intense activity as a painter, marked by the increasing influence of Italian Renaissance art and the transition of Rembrandt's style to one more classical and spiritually introspective. Among the works produced are two versions of *The Holy Family* (Leningrad, Hermitage, 1645; Cassel, Gemäldegalerie, 1646), *The Adoration of the Shepherds* (London, National Gallery, 1646), and the *Young Girl at the Window* (London, Dulwich Picture Gallery, 1645). *The Three Trees*, 1643 (cat. no. 67), *Abraham and Isaac*, 1645 (cat. no. 55), and *Jan Cornelis Sylvius, Preacher*, 1646 (cat. no. 20).

1 6 4 9. Ousts Geertge Dircx from his house and is sued by her for breach of promise. Hendrickje Stoffels, about 23 years old, is first mentioned in the court proceedings, and she and Rembrandt maintain a loving relationship for the rest of her life. They never marry, no doubt at least in part because the artist needs the income from Saskia's estate, which he would lose by remarriage. He completes the etching *The Hundred Guilder Print* (B., Holl. 74).

1 6 5 1. *Clement de Jonghe: Printseller* (cat. no. 23) and *The Goldweigher's Field* (cat. no. 77).

1 6 5 2. Receives the commission for *Aristotle Contemplating the Bust of Homer* (New York, Metropolitan Museum), completed the following year, from the nobleman Don Ruffo of Messina. *Christ Preaching ('La Petite Tombe')* (cat. no. 58) and *Faust* (cat. no. 39).

1 6 5 3. Having placed himself deeply in debt, owing partly to his extensive art collection, Rembrandt finds himself in financial jeopardy in the midst of a general economic depression in Holland. He borrows from several sources, among them his friend Jan Six, the burgomeister of Amsterdam.

1 6 5 4. Rembrandt and Hendrickje are brought before the ecclesiastical authorities for not being married. In October Hendrickje bears Rembrandt a daughter, Cornelia, who is baptized at the Oude Kerk. His financial situation worsens, exacerbated by a change in taste favoring the more classical and elegant styles of several of his former pupils. He paints the *Bathsheba* (Paris, Louvre) and the *Portrait of Jan Six* (Amsterdam, Six Collection). *The Circumcision in the Stable* (cat. no. 60), *The Virgin and Child with the Cat and Snake* (cat. no. 61), and *The Golf Player* (cat. no. 40).

1 6 5 5. *The Goldsmith* (cat. no. 41) and *Abraham's Sacrifice* (cat. no. 63).

1 6 5 6. Not able to meet his financial obligations, Rembrandt obtains from the High Court a "cessio bonorum," effectively placing him in bankruptcy. On July 20, the court orders an inventory and liquidation of his goods, the inventory being carried out on July 25–26. His possessions, including his art collection, are sold for very modest sums in public auctions beginning in September 1656 and continuing through 1658, under the supervision of Thomas Jacobszoon Haaring. *Abraham Entertaining the Angels* (cat. no. 64), his last print on a Biblical theme.

1 6 5 8. *Self-Portrait* (New York, The Frick Collection) and *Negress Lying Down* (cat. no. 43).

1 6 6 0. On December 15, Titus and Hendrickje legally establish a business entity as art merchants, acquiring Rembrandt's artistic production with rights of exclusivity for the purpose of sale. Rembrant effectively becomes their unsalaried employee, provided with room and board. The purpose of the arrangement is to protect him from creditors and from the new, restrictive regulations of the painters' Guild of St. Luke, which had banned him from trade because of his bankruptcy. On December 18, Rembrandt and his family move from the house on the Breestraat, which had been sold in February 1658, transfer being delayed by legal complications. Their new address is a modest home on the Rozengracht, in the quiet district known as the Jordaan, inhabited by artisans and shopkeepers.

1 6 6 1. Paints *The Conspiracy of Claudius Civilis* (Stockholm, Nationalmuseum) for the Burgerzaal of the Niewe Stathuis of Amsterdam. The painting is installed in 1662, but removed the following year. Consequently the work is cut down, probably by the artist himself, for resale.

1 6 6 2. Paints *The Portrait of the Syndics of the Clothmakers' Guild* (Amsterdam, Rijksmuseum).

1 6 6 3. July 21 is the probable date of the death of Hendrickje Stoffels. She is buried on July 24 at the Westerkerk.

1 6 6 5. Executes last etching, *Jan Antonides Van der Linden* (B., Holl. 264). At this period he is working on *The Jewish Bride* (Amsterdam, Rijksmuseum) and *The Prodigal Son* (Leningrad, Hermitage), dated variously between 1665 and 1668.

1 6 6 8. On February 10, Titus marries Magdalena van Loo, the niece of Saskia's sister Titia. Titus dies that same year, on September 4, and is buried at the Zuiderkerk.

OCTOBER 4, 1 6 6 9. Death of Rembrandt van Rijn. He is buried on October 8, in Amsterdam at the Westerkerk.

Bibliography of Works Cited

Clifford S. Ackley, *Printmaking in the Age of Rembrandt.* Boston: Museum of Fine Arts, 1981.

[B.] Adam Bartsch, *Catalogue raisonné de toutes les estampes qui forment l'oeuvre de Rembrandt, et ceux de ses principaux imitateurs.* 2 vols. Vienna, 1797.

[Bartsch] Adam Bartsch, *Le Peintre-graveur.* 21 vols. Vienna, 1802–21.

[Benesch] Otto Benesch, *The Drawings of Rembrandt.* 6 vols. London, 1954–57.

Charles Blanc, *L'Oeuvre complet de Rembrandt décrit et commenté.* 2 vols. Paris, 1859–61.

Karel G. Boon, *Rembrandt: The Complete Etchings.* London, 1963.

Sophie de Bussierre, *Rembrandt: Eaux-fortes.* Paris: Musée du Petit Palais, 1986.

[Churchill] W. A. Churchill, *Watermarks in Paper.* Amsterdam, 1935.

Kenneth Clark, *Rembrandt and the Italian Renaissance.* New York, 1966.

[Gersaint] Edmé-François Gersaint, *Catalogue raisonné de toutes les pièces qui forment l'oeuvre de Rembrandt.* Paris, 1751.

Jacqueline and Maurice Guillaud, *Rembrandt: La Figuration humaine.* Paris: Bibliothèque Nationale, 1987.

[Heawood] Edward Heawood, *Watermarks, Mainly of the 17th and 18th Century.* Monumenta Chartae Papyraceae Historiam Illustrantia, I. Hilversum, Netherlands, 1950.

[H.] Arthur M. Hind, *A Catalogue of Rembrandt's Etchings.* 2nd ed., 2 vols. London, 1923.

[Hind] Arthur M. Hind, *Early Italian Engraving.* 7 vols. London, 1938–48.

[de Jonghe] Cornelis Hofstede de Groot, *Die Urkunden über Rembrandt (1575–1721).* Quellenstudien zur holländischen Kunstgeschichte III (no. 346). The Hague, 1906.

[Hollstein] F. W. H. Hollstein, *Dutch and Flemish Etchings, Engravings, and Woodcuts, ca. 1450–1700.* Amsterdam, 1949–.

[Holl.] F. W. H. Hollstein, *Dutch and Flemish Etchings, Engravings, and Woodcuts, ca. 1450–1700,* vols. XVIII–XIX (Rembrandt van Rijn). Compiled by Christopher White and Karel G. Boon. Amsterdam, 1969.

[de Jonghe]: see Hofstede de Groot

Madlyn Kahr, "Rembrandt's Esther: A Painting and an Etching Newly Interpreted and Dated," *Oud Holland,* LXXXI (1966), pp. 228ff.

[Lieure] Jules Lieure, *Jacques Callot.* 5 vols. Paris, 1924–29.

[Lugt] Frits Lugt, *Les Marques de collections de dessins et d'estampes.* Amsterdam, 1921. *Supplément.* The Hague, 1956.

Charles Henry Middleton, *Descriptive Catalogue of the Etched Work of Rembrandt van Rhyn.* London, 1878.

Ludwig Münz, *A Critical Catalogue of Rembrandt's Etchings.* 2 vols. London, 1952.

Konrad Oberhuber, *Disegni di Tiziano e della sua cerchia.* Venice: Fondazione Giorgio Cini, 1976.

Rembrandt: Experimental Etcher. Boston: Museum of Fine Arts; New York: Pierpont Morgan Library, 1969.

Jakob Rosenberg, *Rembrandt: Life and Work.* 3rd ed. London, 1968.

Jakob Rosenberg, Seymour Slive, and E. H. Ter Kuile, *Dutch Art and Architecture 1600–1800.* Pelican History of Art. Baltimore, 1966.

H. M. Rotermund, "Untersuchungen zu Rembrandts Faustradierung," *Oud Holland,* LXXII (1957), pp. 151ff.

[Röver]: see Van Gelder and Van Gelder-Schrijver

F. Schmidt-Degener, *Catalogus van de Verzameling Etsen van Rembrandt in het bezit van I. de Bruijn.* The Hague, 1932.

Jan Six, "Gersaints lijst van Rembrandts prenten," *Oud Holland,* XXVII (1909), pp. 65ff.

Walter L. Strauss and Marjon Van Der Meulen, *The Rembrandt Documents.* New York, 1979.

W. R. Valentiner, *Die Handzeichnungen Rembrandts.* Klassiker der Kunst. 2 vols. New York, 1925, 1934. (Also Berlin/Leipzig, n.d.)

H. Van de Waal, "Rembrandt's *Faust* Etching: A Soucinian Document and the Iconography of the Inspired Scholar," *Oud Holland,* LXXIX (1964), pp. 7ff.

[Röver] J. G. Van Gelder and N. F. Van Gelder-Schrijver, "De 'Memorie' van Rembrandt's prenten in het bezit van Valerius Röver," *Oud Holland,* LV (1938), pp. 1ff.

J. G. Van Gelder and N. F. Van Gelder-Schrijver, "De Namen van Rembrandt's Etsen," *Oud Holland,* LVI (1939), pp. 87f.

Werner Weisbach, *Rembrandt.* Berlin, 1926.

Christopher White, *Rembrandt and His World.* 2nd ed. Norwich, England, 1966. (Rev. ed.: *Rembrandt.* London, 1984.)

[White] Christopher White, *Rembrandt as an Etcher: A Study of the Artist at Work.* 2 vols. London, 1969.

Christopher White, "Rembrandt's Etching and Drawing of a *Cottage with a White Paling,*" *The Burlington Magazine,* CX, no. 784 (July 1968), pp. 390ff.

[White, Boon]: see Hollstein, XVIII–XIX, 1969.

Pierre Yver, *Supplément au Catalogue raisonné de MM. Gersaint, Helle et Glomy.* Amsterdam, 1756.

Concordances

There are four concordances. The first lists the prints in the Weil collection by title, followed by Hind number, Bartsch/Hollstein number, and the number in this catalogue. The other three list the prints by catalogue raisonné number: first in Hind order, then in Bartsch/ Hollstein order, and finally in the order of this catalogue.

Throughout the concordances the Hind number is given in boldface, the Bartsch/Hollstein number in italic, and the number for this catalogue in regular roman type.

Listing by Hind Number followed by title, Bartsch/Hollstein number, and catalogue number

Listing by Bartsch/Hollstein Number followed by title, Hind number, and catalogue number

Listing by Catalogue Number followed by title, Hind number, and Bartsch/Hollstein number